PAINLESS
PROJECT MANAGEMENT

PAINLESS PROJECT MANAGEMENT

A Step-by-Step Guide for Planning, Executing, and Managing Projects

PAMELA McGHEE
PETER McALINEY

BICENTENNIAL
1807
WILEY
2007
BICENTENNIAL

John Wiley & Sons, Inc.

Published by John Wiley & Sons, Inc., Hoboken, New Jersey.
Published simultaneously in Canada.

Wiley Bicentennial Logo: Richard J. Pacifico

For general information on our other products and services or for technical support, please contact our Customer Care Department within the United States at (800) 762-2974, outside the United States at (317) 572-3993 or fax (317) 572-4002.

Wiley also publishes its books in a variety of electronic formats. Some content that appears in print may not be available in electronic books. For more information about Wiley products, visit our web site at www.wiley.com.

Library of Congress Cataloging-in-Publication Data:

McGhee, Pamela, 1946–
 Painless project management : a step-by-step guide for planning, executing, and managing projects / Pamela McGhee, Peter McAliney.
     p. cm.
  ISBN 978-0-470-11721-7 (pbk.)
 1. Project management. I. McAliney, Peter, 1961– II. Title.
  HD69.P75M3875   2007
  658.4′04—dc22
                                             2007019249
Printed in the United States of America.

10 9 8 7 6 5 4 3 2 1

To Multiple Sclerosis and breast cancer, both of which I have managed using project management, the first as a program consisting of numerous projects and the second as a stand-alone project, temporary work, with a beginning and an *end!*

Pamela McGhee

To the two most important people in my life—my wife Kristan and our daughter Sierra—who have proven that project management is not the sole dominion of the left brained. It is through the efforts of their right-brain managed project (. . . that would be me!) that this book has come to fruition.

Peter McAliney

CONTENTS

If all of the project management books in the world were laid end to end, the line would extend to the moon and back.

Why write another one?

The truth is that most of those books paint project management as really difficult, laden with formulae, revolving around complicated terminology, requiring mastery of all kinds of knowledge areas, bringing a whole new layer of complexity to that poor little word "process."

Project management can be relatively simple and straightforward for the majority of projects. The complexity is not in the process, but in the people and organizational relationships surrounding the planning and execution of projects.

The project management method is not brain surgery and it is not new. It is used when developing a business system, creating a new pharmaceutical product, building an oil rig, or developing a new market for a product.

Project management is required in all industries, businesses, organizations, and disciplines.

Today's business managers and professionals are called on to manage projects at all levels, therefore, project management skills are a requirement for a successful career in business.

Project management is, not so surprisingly, similar from industry to industry, from company to company, from organization to organization. Later in our book, we'll discuss project management as a generic shell—learn it once and apply it forever!

The project manager follows a planned sequence, applies controls, and delivers the required result after first determining just what the client/customer wants and if he can get there with the resources he is willing to expend.

How can this be "painless?" That is what this book is all about. Read on . . .

All forms in this book are copyrighted in print, electronic, and other media. Many of the forms in this book are available for download. To customize these documents for personal use, download them to your hard drive from:

www.painlessprojectmanagement.info.

The documents can then be opened, edited, and printed using Microsoft Word. The available forms appear in the Appendix of this book for easy reference.

THE PAINLESS FASTER, SIMPLER METHOD FOR SMALLER PROJECTS AND NEWER PROJECT MANAGERS

If you are new to project management, have been thrown into a project management role for the first time, have "accidentally" become a project manager, or have been told to "just go do it" without much direction, Part I is for you. We'll take you through the basic steps, in order, like an easy-to-follow recipe. We promise you, the process will be painless.

CHAPTER 1

Introduction to Project Management

Project management is as old as we are. Africans used project management to build the great pyramids. Mayans used project management to build their temples and pyramids. Romans used project management to build aqueducts to carry water from the mountains to their cities. Chinese used project management to build the Great Wall. In fact, almost all important human achievements have required the use of project management.

Project management allows us to control the process and progress of invention. It allows us to apply and keep track of resources needed to produce that new product or service. Project management allows us to gather and harness resources toward a specific end or outcome.

Businesses and organizations have ongoing needs for new products and services to sell or use. These items or services may never have been created before, or they may represent new versions of existing entities. Either way, their creation requires the establishment of a project, and all projects need project management.

To start, we need to define a few of the terms we use throughout the book:

- *Project:* A unique, one-time work effort with a defined start and a defined end, the objectives of which are defined in advance by those who are paying the bill (and those who have vested interests) and are to be achieved by the use of finite and limited resources. Projects are temporary work, bounded by time, resources, and requirements.

- *Project management:* The processes involved in managing a project that requires the application of planning, team building, communicating, controlling, decision making, and closing skills, using specific tools and techniques.
- *Project manager:* The person responsible and accountable for managing a project's planning and performance. He or she is the single point of accountability for a project.
- *Project Management Life Cycle (PMLC):* A series of phases undertaken to deliver a required project outcome (product or service.)
- *Product or service:* The end result of the project undertaken to produce it.
- *Sponsor:* Those responsible for giving rise to, permitting, supporting, and paying for the project.
- *Stakeholder:* Anyone with a vested interest in the outcome of the project. Also those who provide requirements or input as to the project's outcome.
- *Owner:* Those who will own, operate, and maintain the product or service delivered by the project.
- *Client:* Those for whom the project manager is managing the project.

Project management allows us to invent things—products or services that we need or want to have—on a schedule and with control over the process. In the past 20 years or so, businesses and organizations have been producing new and improved products and services at an ever-increasing rate, therefore, project management has become a larger and larger component of businesses, institutions, organizations, and governments.

In a nutshell, a project manager, using the PMLC, delivers a product or service to those who paid for its development. He or she does not deliver the project. The project is only the mechanism of production. The project manager delivers the product or service paid for by the sponsor/stakeholders/clients/owners.

Every project is approached in the same way, all of the time, each time. There is a defined series of steps to go through based on responses to the following issues:

1. Determine what new product or service the sponsor/stakeholders/clients/owners (the bill payers and those with vested interests) want and their willingness to pay for it.
2. Describe a desirable product or service that they can get within an acceptable time frame.
3. Use the planning process to create the specifications of the product or service and to schedule and estimate the cost of its development (called costing).
4. Apply controls and techniques for quality, risks, costs, and changes during the development (execution) of the product or service.
5. Deliver the product or service.
6. After delivery, assess what was done, how well it was done, the degree of client satisfaction with the product or service, and how the process can be improved for the next project.

In addition, don't forget, everyone involved must be kept informed as long as the project is alive—from beginning to end.

The 100,000-Foot View

All projects have similar characteristics. They flow through four main stages (see Figure 1.1), each stage characterized by activities that occur and deliverables that are produced.

A helpful way to think about a project—no matter what type or size—is to build a road map to connect these four stages. Actually,

Stage	Concept ⟹ Plan ⟹		Execute and Control ⟹	Close
Activity	Determine what the business need is	Identify what needs to be done, by whom, and when	Work the plan, refine earlier time and work estimates, deliver the project	Determine what was done well, not so well, and how to do better next time
Deliverables	Business Case	Charter Project Plan	Status Reports	Lessons Learned Document

Definitions	
Business Case	– The proven business justification for the project
Charter	– The agreement governing the size and scope of the project
Project Plan	– The operating plan for the project
Status Reports	– Periodic reports showing progress and challenges facing a project
Lessons Learned Document	– Project recap of lessons that can be employed by subsequent projects

Figure 1.1   Project Flow. © Copyright 2007 Pamela McGhee and Peter McAliney.

you want to build a series of road maps, with each one more detailed than the one before it. Start with Conceptualizing by establishing a Business Case. Then, proceed to Planning. Planning has two major components: (1) writing a Project Charter and (2) developing the actual project plan by defining the work to be done, scheduling it, and costing that work. This is done repeatedly until time and cost estimates are sufficiently refined and validated.

In Executing and Controlling, the project manager primarily oversees and supervises the work required to build the product or service, while handling those unanticipated changes (i.e., "change orders") that pop up in every project and rain down upon every project manager. After the product or service is produced (and tested!), it is turned over to the original sponsor/stakeholders/clients/owners. Is the project over?

No!

After the sponsor/stakeholders/clients/owners have taken possession of their product or service, the project manager, the project team, and the clients (if they can be convinced to do so) conduct the Project Close or Post Mortem phase, the last phase of the PMLC.

This last phase is important because it is where the project manager, the project team, and the clients learn what went well (so they can replicate it) and what went badly (so they don't do it again). In addition, the financial and administrative books are closed, the team members reassigned, and project documentation is completed and filed—accessible to those carrying out future projects so that the process need not be reinvented and future projects can be carried out even better.

The Project Manager's Role

The project manager has multiple roles (Table 1.1). First, project managers are in charge of managing the resources needed to deliver the product of the project, managing the budget and time line, and managing the process. Second, they need to be able to perform the duties of a traditional manager—delegating, negotiating, persuading, organizing, coordinating, facilitating, and team building. Third, they must manage and execute the communications plan—or—more simply to decide what to tell and to whom. Fourth, they must understand the underlying business purpose of the project well enough to make the correct decisions to manage the project's execution.

As far as sponsor/stakeholders/clients and other interested parties are concerned, the project manager must manage in an environment filled with unknowns. These unknowns may include market and business changes occurring during the project, changes in requirements fueled by competing products/services, or horror of horrors, the right people not being involved early on in the project. The project manager cannot necessarily control how the project came to be or who was involved in its inception. At times, projects must be restructured, broken into more than one project, recognizing the existence

Table 1.1   The Project Manager's Multiple Roles

Role	Description	Elements
1	The project management expert	Methodologies
		Basic and advanced project management tools
		Budgeting
2	The quintessential manager	Delegating
		Negotiating
		Persuading
		Organizing
		Coordinating
		Facilitating
		Team building
3	The primary communicator or expert in effective communication	Verbal presentations
		Written reports
		Ad-hoc or spontaneous explanations and elaborations
		Cheerleader
		Marketing
		Training
4	Knows enough about the work to manage its execution	

© Copyright 2007 Pamela McGhee and Peter McAliney.

of a wider (or narrower) stakeholder base. The project manager may have control over the project, but she or he has little control over the environment within which the project takes place.

The project manager is accountable for all project issues, but has precious little authority outside of the project scope—and the owners can even decide to change that scope.

The project manager is accountable for everything relating to the project—responsible for everything and yet has limited authority.

Project managers must continuously balance (or more aptly, juggle) multiple points of view, multiple interests, and a variety of demands—many of which are in conflict. Herding cats comes to mind.

In addition, the project manager must communicate to all interested parties; be responsive; control the details of the project in all of its stages; and monitor costs, time, risk, and quality according to some predetermined standards.

As far as the project team is concerned, the project manager must collaborate with them in every stage of planning and execution to make certain that the agreed-upon plan is being followed. The project manager must make certain that all team members are carrying out their responsibilities—without seeming to be an ogre, control freak, task master, or someone who can be pushed around and ignored.

Who, you might ask, in their right mind, would want to be a project manager? Well, there are rewards. Project management is a valuable technique/skill/talent. It provides several sturdy rungs on a career ladder. And sometimes it's fun. Plus, it generally pays well.

TIP

As a project manager, always put yourself in the client's shoes . . . first, last, and always: **(1) Understand what I want, (2) Give me an early ballpark cost, (3) Find out what I really want/need and what I'll pay for, (4) Give me a more definite cost and time estimate, (5) Build my product, (6) Deliver it when you said you would, and by the way, it would be nice if you could do it better, faster, and cheaper next time.**

Conclusion

In this chapter, we provided the context for project management. Project management is based on a proven methodology and requires a project manager to draw on a number of different skill sets. It is both process oriented and people intensive. (How's that for being able to leap tall buildings in a single bound?) Project management is doable by the normal person with some degree of project knowledge and the ability to walk, chew gum, and communicate at the same time (you do have to keep several balls in the air).

Increasingly, the work that is being done in organizations today requires good project management skills. A knowledge of the project management process and the tools of project management, along with people-management skills, are must-haves for those building their careers in today's workplace.

REAL LIFE EXPERIENCES FROM THE TRENCHES

VIGNETTE I—The Birth of a Project

I was called in to a large consumer products company that wanted to initiate a pilot project between the company and some of its large distributors. It was a tricky situation. While the ultimate quality and service of the product was in the interests of both the company and its distributors, margins across the value chain had been diminished due to an increased competitive environment. Under this duress, both the company and its distributors were competing for the dwindling margin. The situation was causing stress for both the company and its distributors. Based on internal, individual company pressures, each of the parties started to employ business practices that were more in the short-term interest of themselves at the expense of benefiting both parties in the long-term. These continued behaviors led to a loss of trust between both parties to the point where overall product quality and service to their end customer were being compromised. Something had to be done.

The president of the company and three of his distributors agreed to address the issue. In the terminology of project management, they agreed to sponsor a project.

The first task was to bring senior managers of four companies together—the consumer products company and its three distributors—to begin to engage in a dialogue. If senior management is not committed, a project will never get off the ground. To initiate the pilot project that the president of the consumer products company had envisioned, this preliminary meeting needed to be flawless. The meeting would have to result in two deliverables—a working set of shared assumptions by all companies and a first draft Project Charter. The *Project Charter* defines the work, the resources, and the outcomes associated with securing an objective for a company. While project management texts can tell you what needs to be in a Project Charter, they rarely prepare you for all of the human factors that are involved in delivering a completed Project Charter. In this case, the charter needed to be developed in an environment of distrust that had developed over many years. The Project Charter needed to be developed through a collaborative, very deliberate, iterative approach. There were some interesting real-world implications of the two deliverables required in developing the Project Charter for this company. This chartering process really had two deliverables: trust and the charter document itself.

The first deliverable associated with this Project Charter is not addressed in too many books—the acknowledgment that sometimes the working relationships between the companies (in this particular case, or parties in general) required to complete a project is far from perfect. Here, the deliverable is not something you can touch or feel, but rather an *intangible* deliverable. This issue had to be addressed and all parties—stakeholders—had to feel that they were heard. If we were unable to accomplish this first deliverable—trust—the pilot project was a nonstarter. As project manager, I had to identify and call in resources to help me design a meeting that would yield successful attainment of the first deliverable.

The second deliverable—the Project Charter—is much more tangible. However, as I saw in this instance—and many other instances where I have helped develop a Project Charter—the development of a Project Charter is very much a process. And as such, I have not seen two instances where the process was exactly the same. For this case, we designed a two-day off-site meeting where we had the senior managers—the future project sponsor—develop a rough cut of a Project Charter. While it lacked the specificity that is required in a Project Charter, the very process of engaging senior managers in the first revision of the Project Charter helped them to establish the direction of the project they envisioned while at the same time increasing their level of commitment to the initiative. To me, the Project Charter is just as much about deliverables as it is about commitment and communication.

PETER J. McALINEY
CHENERY & CO., Inc.

CHAPTER 2

The Project Management Life Cycle, the Work Cycle, and the Business Context

Project management relies on applying a very specific tool set within an ordered process. This ordered process is called the Project Management Life Cycle (PMLC). The PMLC has a number of variations including some that are proprietary (Agile) and others that are promoted by standards organizations (PMI's PMBOK). Some variations start the cycle earlier than others, other variations use brand-specific terminology and focus on a number of processes. Some use different names for the tools, define them in marginally different ways, and use different symbols to represent the tools in pictorial representations. But, cutting through words and symbols, all healthy projects follow a similar life cycle and use the same basic tool set. Unhealthy projects wander off in any number of different directions. In this chapter, we introduce you to the PLMC, the useful concept of a *Work Cycle* (which is subordinate to and controlled by the PMLC), and the utility of ascertaining the business context (position) of any project you come across in order to better manage that project as well as the associated stakeholders, sponsor, clients, and other interested parties.

Yes, the project manager has to manage them, *and* their expectations, as well.

Project Management Life Cycle

As defined earlier, a project is temporary work that can be viewed as a journey from Start (Concept) to Finish (Close). To make this journey successful, a project needs the previously mentioned ordered processes that can also be called a *road map* (see Figure 2.1). This road map is but another name for the PMLC. The PMLC is a guide, a

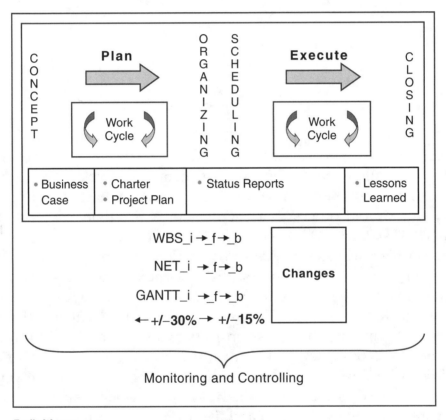

Definitions
_i - Initial estimates
_f - Final estimates, before client sign-off
_b - Baseline (i.e., Final estimates, after client sign-off)

Figure 2.1   The Enhanced PMLC Shell: The Road Map. © Copyright 2007 Pamela McGhee and Peter McAliney.

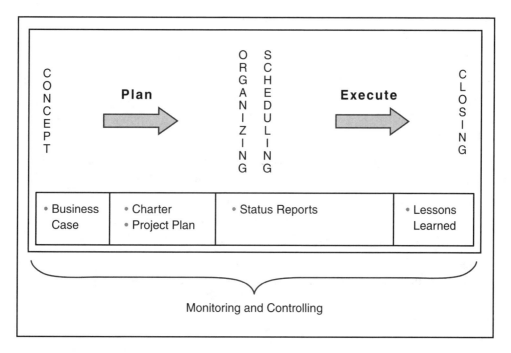

Figure 2.2   The PLMC Shell (I). © Copyright 2007 Pamela McGhee and
Peter McAliney.

template, that comes equipped with a powerful tool kit. This tool-
enhanced template can serve the needs of any size project—from baking a cake to launching a Martian explorer. Figure 2.2 illustrates the
flow of the PMLC. It is the basis for the 100,000-foot view discussed
in Chapter 1.

The Work Cycle

Using the PMLC alone will not ensure a successful project. By itself,
it is inadequate to deliver results. You must deal also with *the work*
that needs to be done to produce the product or service the project
was established to create. To develop any product or service, you must

know the nature of the work to create the end result. For example, to produce an advertising campaign, you need to know about advertising—the work that needs to be done to produce such a campaign. To develop a technology-based business system, you must know about analysis, design, and development work—the work that must be done to deliver a business system to a client. The phases of a Work Cycle will "map" to the PMLC phases, no matter how many phases the Work Cycle may have. Also note that those phases may be iterative.

The process of actually *doing* the work *is* the execution of the *Work Cycle*. The PMLC is merely a shell—a generic shell—a control and change mechanism for all work defined as project work (Figure 2.3). That same shell is used for construction projects, boat building projects, advertising projects, business systems projects—indeed, for all projects (remember, baking a cake or launching a Martian

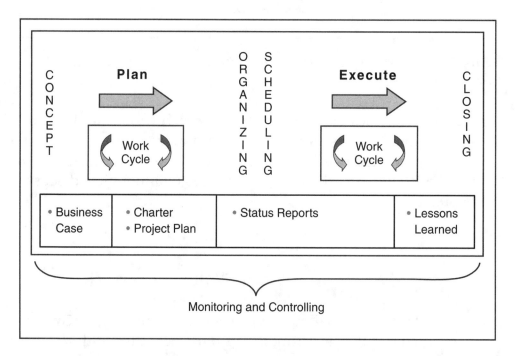

Figure 2.3   The PMLC Shell (II). © Copyright 2007 Pamela McGhee and Peter McAliney.

explorer). It is the Work Cycle controlled by the PMLC that defines a project as a systems project or an engineering project or an advertising project or an IT infrastructure project (Figure 2.4). The Work Cycle defines how to build/create the product or service the project was created to deliver. In Figure 2.3, the Work Cycle and the PMLC are correlated.

Astoundingly, in many project management methodologies and texts, the important Work Cycle is all but ignored. A project is always tied to the product or service that it produces. The manager of such a project must always have some knowledge of the work—the Work Cycle. Some texts define a separate job function called "the professional Project Manager." The tacit assumption is that a "Project Manager" manages projects—all projects. We believe that this model will not yield the best results for an organization. A project manager is always, at some point, tied to the "work." While project

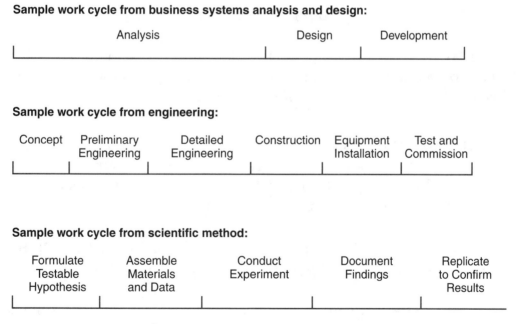

Figure 2.4   Work Cycle. © Copyright 2007 Pamela McGhee and Peter McAliney.

management does require a specific type of knowledge, specific skill sets, and a degree of "talent," a project manager cannot manage a project if she or he knows nothing about the work. Project managers who do find themselves in this unenviable position have to be "quick studies" and/or have a subject matter expert, an advisor, with the subject matter expertise, with whom they must work closely.

TIP

When learning project management, always think about *your* Work Cycle and how project management relates to it. A project manager must understand how to apply project management within the context of her work.

Tools of the PMLC

The PMLC is much more powerful than just a flow manager. It includes powerful tools that are used time and again as the project unfolds, each time with greater precision. These four tools are:

1. The Work Breakdown Structure (WBS)

    A tool that graphically illustrates or outlines the project work to be done (leading to the creation of the product or service) in an organized and hierarchical fashion.

2. The Network Diagram

    A tool that illustrates the order in which tasks will be done. (It can also be thought of as a flow chart that maps task sequences.)

    The network diagram has also been known as a PERT Chart. We will say more about that later.

3. The Gantt Chart (and its derivative—the Cost Spreadsheet)

   A calendar overview of tasks, whereby tasks are mapped against a time line.

   Cost Spreadsheet—Detailed listing of tasks with associated labor and material costs.

4. The Change Control Mechanism

   A system whereby change requests are submitted, prioritized, and acted on (or not) during a project's execution.

We discuss these tools in much greater detail throughout the rest of the book.

These four tools of the PMLC allow the project manager and the project team to define, sequence, and schedule the project with Work Cycle related content. Any other tools that you may use during the project will come from the specific context of the Work Cycle in which the project is being done. As you progress through the PMLC, your ability to use these tools to develop more precise time and material cost estimates becomes greater. Hence earlier in the PMLC, your ability to provide time and budget estimates might be within a plus or minus range of 30 percent (an excellent estimating range after the Project Charter has been drafted and the project manager and team have had a chance to start defining the work that must be done to produce the end produce or service). This 30 percent is a *best case* scenario. To be able to define cost and time to a range of 30 percent this early in the project can indicate: (1) the project and the project team have done a similar project in the past, (2) early planning has been excruciatingly precise and much time/labor (project cost) has been spent, (3) expert advice and counsel (at a project cost) has been sought out by the team early in the project, (4) the team got lucky (Please don't depend on this one!).

As you progress through the PMLC and as you develop a better understanding of the work required, you will be able to develop more precise estimates, perhaps within a range of plus or minus 15 percent (the targeted range for the final estimate, also called the project baseline, against which progress during execution is measured). In some organizations (the project-oriented ones), the plus or minus 15 percent figure is called *Management Reserve*.

In Figure 2.1 on page 16 we illustrate the enhancement of the PMLC by the addition of the associated PMLC tool kit.

Stakeholders and the PMLC

Stakeholders are all those who have a vested interest in the project. As project manager, it is your job to locate and be aware of all of the stakeholders—from high to low—including those who have a vested interest in seeing the project fail (negative stakeholders). Make sure you get them on board early on in the PMLC before you start doing any of the actual work.

TIP

After you have accounted for all stakeholders . . . go back and count them again. A missed stakeholder at the beginning of a project can doom the project to failure.

Project Drivers

While the PMLC provides the processes and corresponding tools for managing a project, a project manager must constantly poll the external environment in three areas—time (schedule), cost (budget), and scope/requirements (totality of work or scope). This is the Project Management Triangle that frames the project manager's decision-making process concerning the project (Figure 2.5).

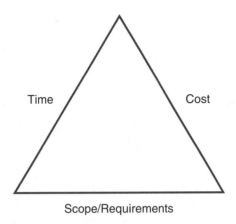

Figure 2.5 The Project Management Triangle. © Copyright 2007 Pamela McGhee and Peter McAliney.

One of the three sides of the triangle will be the primary project driver—the one variable to which the other variables will be subordinated or sacrificed. As the project begins to take form, the project manager will learn what the primary driver is (from the stakeholders). Once understood, she or he must then manage to that driver. There can also be a secondary driver, making the job of managing the project a real balancing act. Take heart, though, because there is no such thing as *three* drivers. If there were three drivers, that would leave nothing to subordinate or sacrifice—no wiggle room.

As project manager, you will often hear stakeholders demanding, "Everything is equally important. Sacrifice nothing." In your project management role of communicator, it is critical that you explain to your stakeholders the impracticality of having three drivers—three drivers would require infinite resources.

TIP

The Project Management Life Cycle cannot stand by itself. It merely controls and regulates, while providing a mechanism for changes and calculating time and costs for the Work Cycle used to produce the end result of the project.

The Project Context

Projects are defined within the context of the organization (see Figure 2.6). As such, they need to be put within the perspective of the specific department and aligned with other business imperatives within the organization. The project manager must be cognizant of how his or her project "fits." Which business areas will be encompassed, or served? What business areas will be affected by this project? What major features will the resulting product or service have and which will it not have. Who will be the primary and secondary recipients of the product/service? Which business areas will be impacted by the project and/or its product? Does this project require input from other projects or products? In other words, what is the

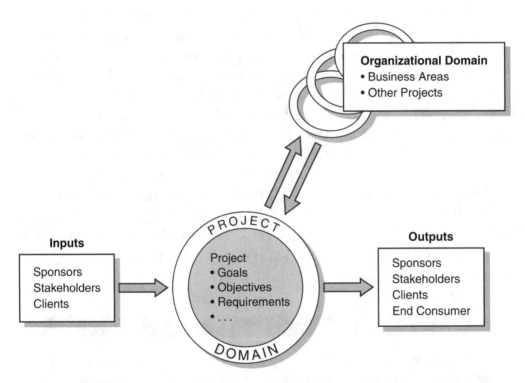

Figure 2.6   Project Context Diagram. © Copyright 2007 Pamela McGhee and Peter McAliney.

business context of this still potential project? Many questions can be answered or at least clarified, through the use of the Project Context Diagram throughout the PMLC.

This Project Context Diagram is an excellent communications tool to use with the sponsor, major stakeholders, minor stakeholders, as well as all other interested parties. It is particularly attractive to upper management because it enables the project manager to provide a big picture view at a glance. (One picture is worth . . .)

Conclusion

The PMLC is the project manager's best friend (actually a life line). Not only is it a clearly defined set of processes, but it also contains a number of powerful tools that, once mastered, will help the project manager and his or her team develop a road map for success. The power of the PLMC is that it is context agnostic (usable from meals to space shuttles). It can accommodate the work—as defined by the Work Cycle—from any functional area within an organization. It is versatile enough to allow for multiple passes of information flow, each pass defining more and more clarity for the project team.

The PMLC is also a powerful communications tool. Not only does it serve as the road map for those associated with a given project—the stakeholders, sponsor, clients, and team members—but also others in the organization who might be impacted by the project. Basic understanding of the PMLC and its associated tools forms a common language for individuals to communicate across organizations. This understanding is becoming increasingly important as workflow across different organizations becomes commonplace in developing products and services for today's global economy and marketplace.

Everyone needs to understand the role project management plays in organizational life. In essence, everyone needs to master the process and tools of project management.

REAL LIFE EXPERIENCES FROM THE TRENCHES

VIGNETTE 2—Project Management: An Undergraduate's Best Friend

Undergraduate work has definitely moved to a model that employs more project-oriented work. I saw this in the several internships I participated in during my time at the City University of New York's Baruch College. While juggling the responsibilities of my class work and the internships, I couldn't help but notice a definite parallel between projects at work and the structure of course work, especially when taking the capstone course in business policy. In both domains, work was becoming increasingly team-based and project-oriented. And, I found that those team-oriented, project-based assignments where we put a plan together, assigned specific duties, established resource commitments, and assessed along the way, tended to be more successful than those for which we did not develop a project plan.

For example, in our business policy course, as a team we were responsible for three discreet team projects and three individual projects (counting the midterm and final as two projects). The professor asked us at the beginning of the term to put together a project plan that would accommodate both the team's work as well as our individual work. He then reviewed the plan with us and made suggestions for improvement, which meant that we would be better assured of the grade we hoped for (an A!). Putting the plan together for the entire term, or project duration, was very helpful in balancing this course (i.e., the project) with other responsibilities I had.

Based on this experience, I believe knowing the fundamentals of project management should be mandatory for anyone entering the business world. Even if you are not managing your own projects, as a new employee, you need to know how to be a more effective team member on a project team. As a recent college graduate, I noticed that students in college, including myself at one point, were not generally very happy when given projects with limited direction from the professor. What we failed to understand was that, in the real world, most projects do not have a clear path which we follow. But, with good project management tools such as planning, executing, controlling, reporting, and communicating tools, we can be successful.

I continue to use the project management skills I learned in my business policy course in my current job with the National Football League (NFL) as a participant of the "Blue Chip" program, a recently launched program designed to provide an elite group of recent college graduates a two-year rotational experience at the New York League office. Every six months, a "Blue Chipper" rotates into a new department within the NFL's business venture departments (Marketing & Sales, Consumer Products, International, and Events). Not surprisingly, participants of the program must be able to hit the ground running in a rapidly changing environment. Presentation skills, project management, continuous improvement, and the ability to be in-the-know are crucial.

ELAINE DELOS REYES
Marketing & Sales "Blue Chipper,"
National Football League

CHAPTER 3

Concept—Building the Business Case

By definition, projects are undertaken by organizations (or individuals) only if they add value or if the resulting product or service is required by law. For added value, to determine if the benefits exceed the costs of undertaking a project, some kind of analysis needs to be made. As mentioned in Chapters 1 and 2, the Project Management Life Cycle (PMLC) is an organized process equipped with powerful tools. The first stage of the PMLC is *Concept*. It is in the Concept stage that the required analysis is performed (see Figure 3.1). It is through the development of the Business Case—the first deliverable of the PMLC—that a project is determined to have value—or not. Someone in the organization—and often it is *not* the individual who will end up as the project manager—must lead an objective analysis of the business situation to determine if a project is really needed (more on how the project manager receives and interprets this initial analysis later).

Concept: Beginning the Process

Every project starts the same way, with a Concept. An individual in an organization has an idea that a project he or she envisions will

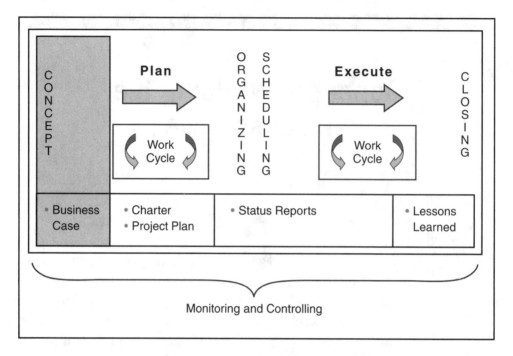

Figure 3.1   Project Management Life Cycle. © Copyright 2007 Pamela McGhee and Peter McAliney.

increase the value that an organization can deliver—whether it is saving time, reducing cost, or increasing quality. This individual, an individual who at a later point may be the project sponsor, will ask someone in the organization to determine what it would take to implement the idea. In the language of project management, the project sponsor is asking for the first deliverable of the PMLC—the Business Case.

The first thing to remember is that not all projects should be attempted. Wait a minute, this is a book about project management! How is it possible that just as we are starting to discuss how to manage a project, the first piece of advice might be "don't do the project?"

Many projects have the potential to be a waste of the organization's time and resources. Remember, the power of the PMLC is that it is an objective process. The function of the Concept stage is to weed out bad projects. This means eliminating the unprofitable, the un-wise, the pet, the frivolous, and the "money-would-be-better-spent-elsewhere" types of projects. When projects spontaneously emerge in an organization, there is a higher probability that they will fail. In fact, about 60 percent of all project ideas should be aborted for reasons of insufficient profitability, not in line with our strategic plan, not in our line of business, too risky, don't have the resources, and other such reasons. Only about 40 percent of projects actually pass the muster of profitability, market advantage, a new line of business necessity, legal requirement, or other valid business rationales that will actually add value to the organization.

How does the weeding out process start? First, by working with the potential sponsor and stakeholders, the issue or problem to be addressed is defined. What are the goals? What are the benefits for such an effort on which corporate resources will be expended? If the project manager is shepherding this process, a visual approach (the use of flip charts and colored markers or a projected laptop screen and fast keying) with stakeholders sponsor group interaction can be useful as a catalyst for problem/issue definition, and so on. Different stakeholders may have different definitions of the problem, or different goals or benefits. At this point, the potential project may split into two or more projects. Defining the objectives (what is the purpose or purposes of this venture) requires a similar teasing out. If the project manager is appointed at this time, persistence and "cutting fat from bone" will be skills he or she uses.

If no project manager has yet been assigned (more often the case), the sponsor and stakeholders will have to do all of this work. When the project manager is brought on board, due diligence requires that he or she check the work—at the very least. This checking will familiarize the project manager with the players, the ideas, and the politics. This is crucial for both survival and project success.

The Business Case allows business management to determine the reach and value of the project, and whether the potential project is a sound business investment.

Developing a Business Case

First, the project manager does not always start with developing the Business Case. By right, it is the responsibility of the sponsor and stakeholders to evaluate the potential project as to the business value of the product or service created and whether the return on investment (ROI) is acceptable. If the product of the project is of value to the organization, the project is given the go-ahead and an official project manager is appointed. This is how it is *supposed* to work.

It actually works this way less than 20 percent of the time. More often than not, the project manager is told to "go do it," often with little direction. That is when the project manager starts to bring definition to the undefined. A dependable way to start is to begin at the business level and start uncovering the true nature of the project "request."

TIP

When assuming the role of project manager, insist on seeing the Business Case. Projects that are "green lighted" without a solid Business Case have a higher probability of failure. Taking the time up front to further vet the Business Case is a wise investment and can reduce the potential for project (and project manager) failure.

In the Concept stage, the potential project manager—at this point, in the role of investigator—works with the clients, sponsor, and major stakeholders to establish a Business Case for the potential project. The Business Case needs to include clear, articulate definitions of:

- The issue or problem to be addressed/solved;
- The goals and benefits of undertaking such a project;
- The objectives of the project;
- The needs and wants;
- The potential project scope;
- The risks and impacts associated with the project;

- The cost benefit analysis; and
- The return on investment.

Because in many organizations, the responsibility of building the Business Case may not be the job of the project manager, in the following discussion, we refer to the role of the individual building the Business Case as the *investigator*.

Issue or Problem to Be Addressed/Solved

The first thing that must be done is to develop clarity around the problem to be addressed/solved. To do this, the investigator will want to get access to the major stakeholders and/or the person who brought the project up in the first place. She needs to pick their brains to determine exactly what goal they had in mind. Collectively is best, but one by one will do if the investigator can't get them all in the same room or on the same conference call at the same time. Ask them to talk about the issue or problem that this potential project would solve. Remember, it's not a project *yet*. The more times the investigator mentions this during this stage the better the expectations around the project will be in the long run.

The major players are not the only individuals in the organization with whom the investigator will want to speak. The investigator will want to go down the chain of command—as low as feasible—and talk to those who are possibly dealing with the issues in the workplace. But remember—it may be neither practical nor politic to get to them. Use good business judgment. Project management has the potential to be highly political (in fact, it almost always is).

TIP

Don't forget the stakeholders who are low on the chain of command when developing the Business Case. They often have a better handle on requirements than management.

Goals and Benefits

Ask all players, "What do you require as an *end result*? How will this benefit the organization, or your department(s), or you?" This may sound corny, but one of the best ways to do this is to drag in a flip chart and have a pocket full of magic markers. Proof of commitment is when the players commandeer the flip chart and markers and start writing themselves.

Objectives

"Why are we embarking on this effort?" "How will we know if we're successful?" Note to the curious—the investigator will probably get the magic marker here—be a willing scribe.

Needs and Wants

Next, Needs and Wants must be tackled. A simple template like the one in Table 3.1 can be used to capture the Needs and Wants of the requestors.

To use this approach, call a short meeting—call it a Project Focus Meeting—of the project sponsor and major stakeholders. Start with a blank flip chart and some colored broad-tipped markers. List the sponsor and the attending stakeholders in the client section and put a date on the flip chart. Draw a line down the middle of the page, putting Needs on the left side and Wants on the right.

Have the meeting attendees list what they *must have* (Needs) in the potential product or service to be produced by the project. Also have them list their *nice to haves* (Wants). When there is a reasonable size list of both, attach order of magnitude costs to fulfill each Need and Want. If the investigator is knowledgeable and fast on his or her feet, he or she can come up with a dollar amount right there in the meeting (very impressive). If not, the investigator will need to figure it out and present the costs in a second meeting.

Table 3.1 Needs and Wants Template

Needs versus Wants List Date: _____

Sponsor: _____

Needs:			Wants:	
1. _____	$ _____		1. _____	$ _____
2. _____	$ _____	+	2. _____	$ _____
3. _____	$ _____		3. _____	$ _____
Total =	$ _____		Total =	$ _____

Stakeholder 1: _____

Needs:			Wants:	
1. _____	$ _____		1. _____	$ _____
2. _____	$ _____	+	2. _____	$ _____
3. _____	$ _____		3. _____	$ _____
Total =	$ _____		Total =	$ _____

Stakeholder N: _____

Needs:			Wants:	
1. _____	$ _____		1. _____	$ _____
2. _____	$ _____	+	2. _____	$ _____
3. _____	$ _____		3. _____	$ _____
Total =	$ _____		Total =	$ _____
Grand Total =	$ _____		Grand Total =	$ _____

Minimum budget and scope for potential project

Maximum budget and scope for potential project

Once the audience of the potential sponsor and stakeholders has generated a list of Needs and Wants and the investigator has established an order of magnitude cost for each, add up all of the costs for the Needs. This total represents the minimum cost of the potential project with the corresponding minimum scope. Then, add up the costs of the Wants and add that to the Needs total. This monetary figure represents the maximum cost and the combined list defines the maximum scope of the potential project.

WARNING!

Do not let the figures be construed as the project's budget. It is far too early to generate a budget. These numbers represent only the inner and outer limits of possible costs. These figures are WAGS (Wild A%# Guess).

TIP

An added benefit of the Needs and Wants list is that it provides the foundation for the high-level requirements needed to draft the project plan.

Preliminary Project Scope

Even at this early stage, what is to be included and what is not to be included in the potential project must be highlighted. How is project scope defined? First, determine, with the sponsor and the stakeholders, what is to be included in the project and what is excluded or is out of bounds. Develop a map of the business real estate (what and who will be involved) to be covered by the potential project.

It is important to make a definitional distinction about scope at this point. A project's scope has two elements:

1. From a business perspective, scope can address the aspect of how many parts of the organization—or entities outside the organization—the project will touch. A project may directly touch only in-

dividuals within a small part of the organization or it may touch many departments as well as entities outside the organization.

2. From a project perspective, scope addresses the totality of the work that must be done to deliver the final results (all deliverables). In very real terms, scope *is* the totality of the Work Breakdown Structure (WBS). If it is not in the WBS, it will be neither built nor delivered. In addition, it won't be budgeted for (costed).

At this point, it is helpful to use a Context Diagram (Figure 3.2, which is the same as Figure 2.6 on page 24) as an aid in understanding and further developing the scope of the project, both from a business perspective and from the project perspective of encompassing all of the work that the project manager must manage and have accomplished.

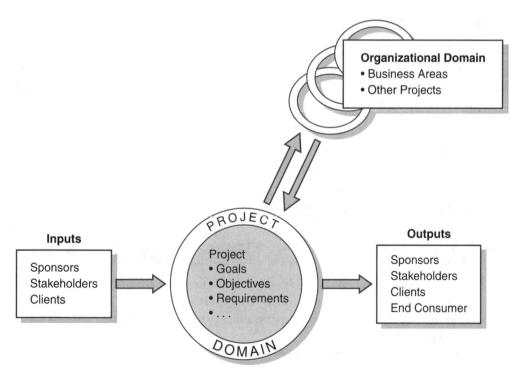

Figure 3.2 Project Context Diagram. © Copyright 2007 Pamela McGhee and Peter McAliney.

It is also helpful to develop the Project Context Diagram with the sponsor and major stakeholders, the project manager acting as a discussion facilitator, to illuminate further requirements and perhaps to delete others that, when seen in the light of open discussion, retreat in importance.

At this point in the proceedings, the more discussion, debating, reality-testing, the better.

In general, there is *some* correlation between small real estate—small project, large real estate—large project. However, it is important to recognize that large does not always mean mission critical. This will be important later on when the project gets going. A project manager leading a large project touching many people may have difficulty getting the attention of people because it is not seen as being important or mission critical.

Risk and Impact

The savvy investigator must be very diligent in leading the sponsor and stakeholders through a rigorous examination of risks. Conducting a risk analysis needs to be a two-way process. The sponsor and stakeholders need to press the investigator on potential areas that they identify as risky just as the investigator needs to press the sponsor and stakeholders on areas that he or she thinks may carry some element of risk. The important thing is that no stone is left unturned—as ugly as it may be. It is important to recognize *everything* that could potentially impact the execution of a project.

TIP

When developing the risk analysis, develop a checklist that includes potential business, technical, societal, legal, and market risks. You will also want to determine if there are any other unique "gotcha" areas that need to be quantified as risks.

Once the risks are identified, they need to be evaluated. A useful tool to help drive the conversation around risk is the Risk/Impact

Analysis Grid (see Figure 3.3). The horizontal axis represents Impact (i.e., the positive or negative value that the project will bring to the organization), from high to low. The vertical axis represents Risk (i.e., the project fails, the project is wildly successful), from low to high. The corresponding internal graph space is divided into quadrants:

- The top left quadrant is high risk, high impact;
- The bottom left, low risk, high impact;
- The top right high risk, low impact; and
- The bottom right, low risk, low impact.

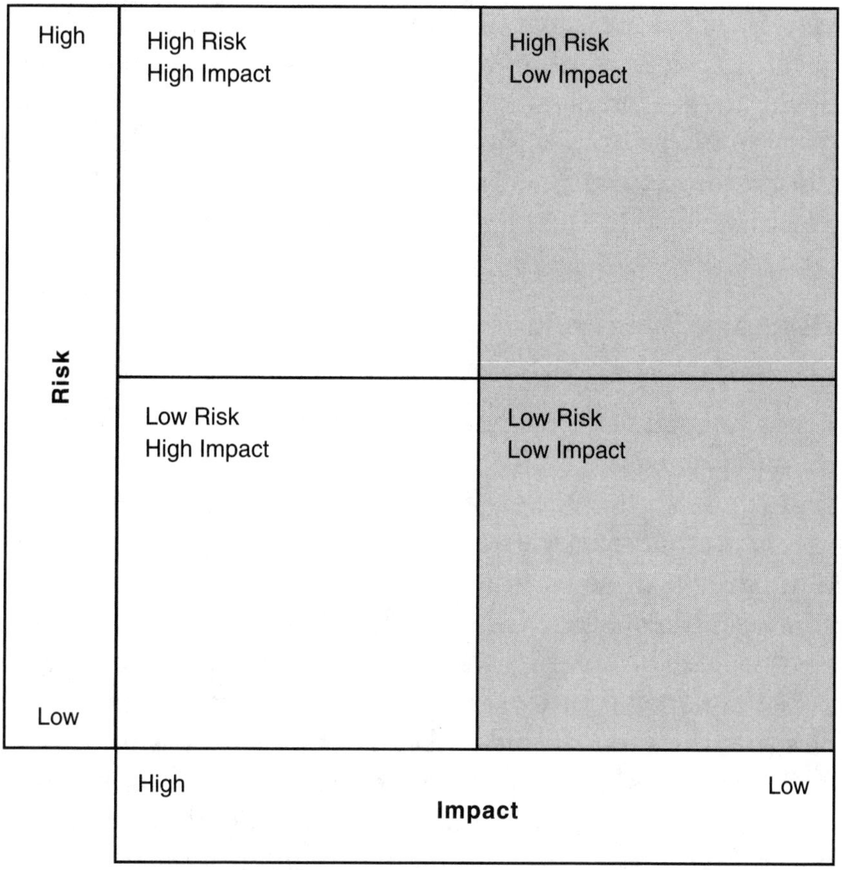

Figure 3.3 Risk/Impact Analysis Grid. © Copyright 2007 Pamela McGhee and Peter McAliney.

Of course, the ideal project would fall into the low risk, high impact quadrant—giving the "most bang for the buck." However, projects that fall into the other categories must often be initiated. A high risk, high impact project may be a mission critical one. A high risk, low impact project may be the result of governmental regulations (like Sarbanes-Oxley). A low risk, low impact project may be the pet project of a key executive or a "nice to have if time and resources permit" project.

The project manager works with the sponsor and stakeholders to place the project on the grid using a number of perspectives (as noted previously—business, technical, societal, legal, market, etc.). A separate point may be plotted for each criterion, creating a type of scatter diagram of Risks and Impacts. The cumulative Risks and Impacts of the project will determine how the project will be managed later on, even down to the precision (granularity) of the Work Breakdown Structure. Items falling in the right shaded area are the projects demanding the most scrutiny. This is where the 60 percent of projects failing to make a solid Business Case are often located.

Cost Benefit Analysis

To find out if the result of the project is worth undertaking, the investigator needs to conduct a Cost Benefit Analysis. It's best to find out the benefits—and what they will cost you—early on. It is in the Concept stage that the first, high-level project costs or numbers are developed. It may seem premature because no one has all the detailed information needed to develop these estimates, but the process of having this conversation with the sponsor, stakeholders, and other interested parties at this point begins to get real numbers on the table. These estimates need to be developed for the work that must be done to produce the deliverables that the sponsor and stakeholders say they want.

How are costs developed? One way to develop these early estimates is to look at the results of past projects that were similar. If your organization is a project management oriented organization, these estimates should be fairly easy to obtain. By looking at what similar projects cost, and making adjustments to reflect the particular needs of the proposed project, the investigator can lead a conversation with the sponsor and stakeholders that will result in initial estimates.

Another way to develop early estimates is to use the Needs and Wants costs (see Table 3.1). With the sponsor and stakeholders, determine which of the Needs and Wants will be in the proposed project. Estimate the dollar costs of each Need and Want and do the arithmetic. This will allow the project manager to give early minimum and maximum costs and time for the potential project.

Do not allow this WAG (Wild A#% Guess) to be construed as the final project budget. The sponsor and stakeholders want some estimated numbers based on very limited knowledge of the desired end results. The investigator needs to be sure he or she manages the potential sponsor and other stakeholder expectations about the firmness and accuracy of these numbers. While the estimate should not be orders of magnitude off, it also cannot be carried to multiple decimal points indicating more accuracy than is possible at this stage. Because both Needs and Wants are used to generate these initial numbers, it is best that they are presented as a range.

The Project Estimating Funnel is a communications tool that is helpful in managing the conversation among the investigator, the sponsor, and stakeholders (see Figure 3.4). It shows the progression from early, less accurate estimates in the Concept stage to the estimates that will eventually be generated in the Planning stage if the Business Case is proven in the Concept stage.

TIP

If the sponsor and stakeholders collectively jump up and down demanding a cost *now*—this minute—tell them if they can be patient and let you finish your investigation, you will be able to provide a more accurate—and workable—estimate. Remind them that the earlier the estimate is made, the less information to make that estimate is available, and the less likely that estimate will be accurate.

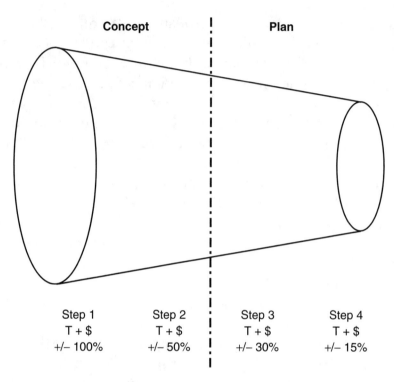

Figure 3.4   Project Estimating Funnel. © Copyright 2007 Pamela McGhee and Peter McAliney.

Return on Investment Analysis

It is possible at this early stage to develop ROI figures, but they will be only of the most general sort. If the cost of the project is estimated at a million dollars and the payback period is three years, the cash flow will not turn positive until year three and one day. Could a better investment of money be made?

As you may surmise, this becomes more than iffy and possibly a useless exercise at this level for all but the most advanced organization. The investigator can probably safely stay out of the ROI exercise and leave it to the business sponsor and stakeholders. If the investigator is pressed to provide an ROI, however, he or she needs to make sure that it is well qualified.

The Business Case and Strategic Alignment

One thing we did not discuss: An important part of the Business Case is how the proposed project aligns with the overall Vision and Mission Statement of the organization. Just as an organization has a Mission Statement, a project should have a Mission Statement. Look through all of the components and discuss with the sponsor and stakeholders the development of a Mission Statement for the project. This should be an independent exercise. Once the Mission Statement has been articulated, it can be checked for alignment with the overall organization.

The project management oriented organization applies project management methodologies and culture from the top down. In such organizations, all selected projects are strategically aligned according to the organization's strategic plan. No project should be selected or assigned resources if it is not in line with that strategic plan (Figure 3.5).

To validate if a project is aligned with the organization's strategic plan, the investigator should start with the organization's Vision and Mission Statements. Sometimes there will be both a Vision and a Mission Statement. Sometimes they are combined. It is the organization's Vision and Mission Statements that capture the highest level purpose of the enterprise. The statements are often printed in the annual report or on the organization's website.

The project next needs to be aligned with more specific goals and objectives. Working down through the organization, it must be aligned with the divisional goals and objectives, and then with the functional goals and objectives within the division. For those organizations that practice a project management portfolio approach, the project must also be aligned with the project portfolio (or program portfolio).

All of the components of the Business Case have been assembled. The proposed project mission has been checked for alignment with the organization. It is now time for the investigator to write

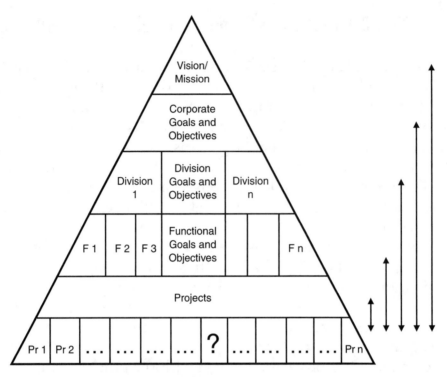

Figure 3.5 The Strategic Alignment of Projects. © Copyright 2007 Pamela McGhee and Peter McAliney.

up the Business Case. Depending on the organization, this may take the form of a slide presentation or a formal report. The Business Case should be a concise representation that enables decision makers in the organization to decide if it is a project that will bring increased value to the organization in the long term (see Table 3.2). Invariably, even with all of the checking and double-checking, phone calls, e-mails, and other communication, there will be areas that will need clarification. It is important to acknowledge any areas that still require direction because this information will be needed by the decision makers to make their final decision.

Table 3.2   Business Case Outline

Business Case Overview
   Proposed project
   Principal investigator(s)
   Contributors
   Project mission

Proposed Project Details
   The issue or problem to be addressed/solved
   The goals and benefits of undertaking such a project
   The objectives of the project
   The needs and wants
   The potential project scope
   The risks and impacts associated with the project
   The cost benefit analysis
   The return on investment (ROI)

How the Project Supports
   Corporate vision/mission
   Corporate goals and objectives
   Division goals and objectives
   Functional goals and objectives
   Project portfolio (if applicable)

Feedback Requested
   Areas for clarification
   Decision

A Disclaimer

What if strategic alignment is not the mantra of your organization? Well, extract the most accurate and clear project Mission Statement from the sponsor and stakeholders and proceed with the Business Case and, if accepted, then with the Project Charter.

The Project Context Diagram will be especially important because it can be used in part as a justification for the project.

While a Business Case is an integral part of the project management process, there are situations in which a Business Case can, and should be bypassed.

There are some ad hoc and exploratory projects for which a Business Case may not be applicable. (Of particular note is the Post-it notes tale from "Real Life Experiences . . .")

Conclusion

Congratulations, the Business Case is now ready for presentation.

The deliverable from the Concept stage of the PMLC is the Business Case. This is the output of a thorough process, whereby an investigator—who may or may not be the appointed project manager—gathers information from the potential sponsor and relevant stakeholders. Initial estimates are developed and scrubbed as the investigator works his or her way through the Concept stage. The investigator must look at the potential project upside down, inside out, and sideways and must check for its alignment from the organization's Mission and Vision Statements to the specific needs of the functional area where the project will be executed.

A Business Case may show that a project does not make sense for an organization. It may be hard to deliver this news to the sponsor who may be very excited about a potential project. The Business Case will not lie if all contributors provide their best estimates as they work through the process. It is better not to start a project that does not add value than to try to force the issue and realize it later after the organization has committed resources to it.

REAL LIFE EXPERIENCES FROM THE TRENCHES

VIGNETTE 3—Why Go to the Trouble of Developing a Business Case?

Below is a White Paper written by Neville Turbit, a Principal of Project Perfect.

www.projectperfect.com.au

An Alternative to the Business Case

by

Neville Turbit

Overview

It is generally accepted that a new project requires a business case to get approval to proceed. The business case is a financial estimate, and justification for the existence of the project. So is it always the best way to agree a project should proceed? This white paper examines an alternative way of thinking. It focuses on two non business case reasons—Innovation and Survival.

Accuracy of the Business Case

It will come as no surprise if I were to say that some numbers in Business Cases are rubbery. It would probably come as no surprise to say that many are downright lies.

I worked for an organisation once that had an office in a street called Foveaux Street. We invented the "Foveaux Forecasting System." When asked for a projection of cost, volumes, growth, records, or even football scores, we would look out the window, read the number plate of the first car we sighted, and adjust the decimal point. If asked for a growth rate, and the first car passing was "ABC 123," we would estimate 12.3%. Sometimes I think business cases would benefit from this approach.

If the business case is so inaccurate, should we be putting so much emphasis on inventing numbers that are baseless? Should we be doing calculations on assumptions that are so vague as to be meaningless? Perhaps ROI (Return on Investment) is not the right criteria in all cases.

The Big Picture

An organisation usually has some goals, or a corporate vision. Usually it is somewhat vague. It is not about quantification but more about direction. It is not about statistical measures but more about what the management wants the company to be. It is about creating initiatives that contribute towards the direction of the company.

Should projects be approved for the same reasons? Should there be a justification to move forward because it is contributing towards an initiative in an unquantifiable way?

Reputation for Innovation

I was recently talking with the CEO of a significant international IT organisation. She told me that she approved a number of internal projects each year that did not have a justifiable return on investment. One of her reasons was that she wanted to employ the best and brightest in her organisation. In order to do this, she needed to provide a creative challenge for them. She needed to stimulate them to use groundbreaking technology.

As she said, perhaps one out of three projects delivered a financial benefit to the organisation. The other two were either abandoned, or at best broke even. The real benefit came from what the people learned, and were able to apply to other projects. It came from retaining the services of bright people who were able to do a better job than more middle of the road workers. It came from having people motivated and productive.

Her organisation was an early leader in Java. When .NET it started to catch on, it was ahead of the market. The new business it generated more than paid for the few failed projects. The premium people were prepared to pay to implement these technologies, funded the experimentation.

Business Cases That Would Fail

Here are a number of business cases that would never have passed the first review.

- Art Fry who worked for 3M came up with sticky paper notes. The idea never made it past the first review. How could you justify the potential of Post-it notes? Where was the business case?

  He used a great approach. He made a batch and passed them out to all the secretaries. When the notes ran out, and the secretaries demanded more, he told them to talk with their bosses. It would be a brave boss who told his secretary that there was no future in Post-it notes and she couldn't have any more.

- How solid was the business case for Michael Dell when he wanted to bypass the accepted supply chain and go direct to consumers. Furthermore, he wanted people to pay for a PC before it was built.

Neither of these would ever get up as a business case however they still worked. The underlying assumptions are just too fantastic to be treated seriously.

Robert D. Shelton, Vice President with the former Arthur D. Little consulting firm includes the ROI question in his symptoms of an anaemic internal market for creativity and innovation. He says that organisations that use only capital-return tools such as ROI or discounted cash flow tend to have a weak innovation culture. "Moreover," he states, "Appropriate measures don't exist to evaluate creativity or potential projects in which there is uncertainty or ambiguity."

Projects for Innovation

Perhaps the answer is that the organisation should take a venture capital approach to some projects each year. If we were investing our personal funds, we might take most of our investments with a guarantee of stable returns, and a few risky investments with the potential for big returns.

An organisation is no different. If the organisation wants stability, they can focus on projects with guaranteed benefits. Avoid any risky projects. They will probably grow with the market, but not gain much advantage. If they want to outgrow the market, part of their project portfolio needs to be in the risky area.

A venture capitalist will invest in a number of companies knowing that the few wins will outweigh the failures. A company that wants to use IT to advantage needs to fund a number of risky projects. That is the only way they will get ahead of their competitors.

Diversify the Risk

Putting all your eggs in one basket is likely to mean you end up with scrambled eggs. It is better to diversify the risky projects and take a different approach to justification. For example, your technology people may propose a project to develop a program that can be integrated with a browser on a client's desktop to advise them of price changes for your products. There is nothing available off the shelf that will do this. The way to start is to fund a proof of concept on a small scale. If it succeeds, perhaps you fund a trial in one region. With that experience, a business case becomes a possibility.

If you adopt this approach, you may find you can fund a number of initiatives that prove the concept before considering the business case. If the organisation invests a proportion of the IT budget in seeking out competitive advantage, perhaps they will find it. If they invest nothing, they can be assured they will not find innovative ways to use IT. It becomes a commodity.

Most organisations invest in market testing new products and services. Why not new IT services? The company accepts that a few marketing concepts will fail, but they need to develop a number in order to find a winner. So with IT. Some concepts will fail, and that is all right. The ones that succeed will make the exercise worthwhile.

Case Study

I spoke with a shipping company some time ago. In their niche market, all the competitors were running the same freight management package with minor variations. Although it could not be cost justified, this company had built their own system over the years which allowed customers to more easily process freight through Customs. This was the main competitive advantage for their organisation. Their growth was almost completely attributed to a computer program.

There had been no business case to develop the system. It had grown over many years but the IT Manager had some bright people and he encouraged them to come to him with development ideas. The company had a culture of innovation and encouraged him to experiment.

He had a budget to fund the ideas without having to go through formal approvals. Sure they had some failures and he had to write off a few projects. The successes more than compensated for the failures yet he said none would ever have seen the light of day if they had to withstand a rigorous business case evaluation.

Stifling Innovation in IT

Some of the brightest people I have ever met have been in the IT industry. Unfortunately, very few work for corporations. They tend to be out there creating games or doing clever stuff on the Web. The corporate IT area typically imposes a straight jacket which limits the bounds of innovation.

If you implement suggestions for innovative IT solutions, you will tap into the problem solving psyche that usually exists in an IT person. I had one situation where we identified an 18-month project to build a new system to handle investment products. The existing system was corrupting data and current values had to be manually calculated. We couldn't even send out statements.

I had a systems analyst who was a handful to manage. He was always going outside the bounds of his role and often creating a great solution to the wrong problem. He came to me and said he could put together a temporary solution using an obscure programming language he had discovered. It would verify if the data was corrupt or not, and if not, calculate the current value. There was no guarantee of success. It defied all the architectural standards. The cost was unable to be calculated. In fact a business case was not even a remote possibility.

In spite of the corporate guidelines, I believed if it could be done, this guy could do it. We gave him the go ahead and put a budget together to cover his cost for three months.

He worked day and night. On occasions he had to be escorted from the building because he was almost asleep at his desk. Suddenly he had a pet project which was using his skills to the full. In three months he built the system. For the balance of the conversion project, we were able to supply about half the policies' current values from the interim system, and identify where the corrupt data was on the other half.

The cost and time savings to administration staff were enormous. An innovative approach allowed us to overcome a major corporate obstacle and in the end there was an ROI. It could have failed but the upside of the project far out-weighed the downside. IT Innovation triumphed.

Without a Business Case

There are already exceptions to the mandatory business case process. Some projects are driven by legislation (think Basil II in the banking industry). There may be no financial return, but they just have to be done.

Others are driven by keeping up with the competitors. It is not so much that the project will provide a competitive and financial advantage. It is more that it will keep you in the game. Don't implement the change, and you will be out of business.

Postponing Major Upgrades

A company reluctantly accepts that they need to devote part of their IT budget to mandatory projects. Whilst some are driven by legislation, others may be driven by lack of support for older systems, network upgrades, new premises, expansion or contractions of their operation. Unfortunately, the usual name of the game is "Postponing the Inevitable." Everyone knows it is coming one day but you keep putting it off. My advice is to forget the business case. Just do it.

Risk of focusing on the Business Case

Looking at the situation from a corporate perspective, what is the cost to the organisation of delaying? What is the cost of running an old and inefficient system rather than replacing it three years earlier with a newer system? What opportunities are lost? What is the drain of staff supporting an old system? If you lose key staff due to the view that their skills are not being upgraded, how will that impact a conversion?

The Questions to Ask

Rather than ask the ROI on a project, here are a few other questions to ask.

- At our present rate of rolling out new IT, where will we be in five years time? What will be the cost of catching up? Can we fund it in one lump sum?
- Are we providing enough new technology experience to our staff to keep them interested, educated and motivated? Are we happy with high staff turnover?
- How well can we answer questions about new technology if we don't use it? Do we have the experience to make the best decisions for our company's IT development?
- From our competitor's point of view, what will they do to pass us in their IT services?
- If I was a competitor, and had to focus on IT as a competitive tool, how would I put us out of business?
- What new technology might eventually put us out of business if we don't implement it?
- What IT services will we need to provide in the future, and how will we get the experience to provide those services?
- If we do upgrade some time in the future, can we guarantee the key staff who have the business knowledge will still be around?
- Can we see a window of time in the future where we can focus an area of the company on upgrading the system, or is now as good a time as any?

All these questions are not about undertaking a project because it has a two-year payback period. They are about surviving.

Summary

It is a fact of life that most projects are approved based on a business case. This is probably the most sensible approach for the bulk of projects as long as someone is held responsible for achieving the benefits. On the other hand, if an organisation is innovative, they should look to running some projects without a business case.

Mix the portfolio with a few risky ventures that may allow the organisation to leap ahead of your competitors. Treat it as new product development. You might end up with a Post-it note or you might end up with a flop. If you don't try, you will end up with nothing. ROI is not a good measure for innovation. Fund innovation separately.

When it comes to IT contributing to the survival of the organisation, it is not about how little you can spend today. NASA tried that and it didn't work. It is about keeping up with the opposition so they can't use IT to put you out of business. It is about using survival as a lever to leapfrog the opposition. It is about not delaying work because now is not a good time. Will tomorrow be any better?

Always judging projects by their business case is for the prudent. Taking a decision that is innovative is for the bold. What sort of organisation do you want to work for?

References

Thanks to an article by Joyce Wycoff who is a co-founder of the InnovationNetwork, an organization focused on helping organizations develop a core competency of innovation. She has a broad background in management and marketing and a deep understanding organizational innovation. Joyce is the author of several books on innovation and creativity, including *Mindmapping, Transformation Thinking,* and *To Do . . . Doing . . . Done!*

Neville Turbit has had over 15 years experience as an IT consultant and almost an equal time working in Business. He is the principal of Project Perfect. Project Perfect is a project management software consulting and training organization based in Sydney, Australia. Their focus is to provide creative yet pragmatic solutions to Project Management issues.

CHAPTER 4

Planning the Work and Working the Plan

The Business Case has passed muster. The project is green lighted. A project manager is appointed—sometimes it's the investigator, but usually it's not. That project manager is you. In this chapter, we cover the project manager's and the project team's responsibilities in *Planning, Execution,* and *Close.*

Planning

First, let's look at the big picture for Planning. The project manager starts by working with the sponsor and major stakeholders to establish a Project Charter. After the Charter is drafted, the project manager and the project team begin the definition of the work (Work Breakdown Structure, WBS) needed to produce the desired product or service. To develop a schedule, a sequence of tasks to be done is created (network). From that logical sequence, a calendar schedule (Gantt Chart) is developed. Figure 4.1 gives an overall picture of the Planning phase.

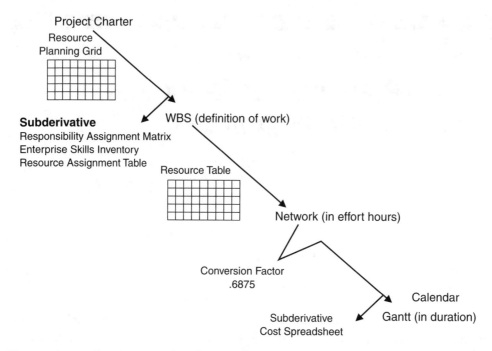

Figure 4.1   The Essentials of a Project Plan. © Copyright 2007 Pamela McGhee and Peter McAliney.

You now lead a newly formed team in Planning (which includes organizing and scheduling), Executing, and, upon completion, celebrating success and Closing the project—the remaining three stages of the Project Management Life Cycle (PMLC; see Figure 4.2). You will begin to appreciate the power of the PMLC as you lead the team through Planning to develop the Project Charter and finally, the Integrated Project Plan (IPP.)

During Planning, the associated Work Cycle is also in operation and is used to conduct an "as is" analysis, requirements definition and analysis, the creation of the "to be" situation (i.e., specifying and designing the product or service to be delivered). Subject Matter Experts (SMEs) in the Work Cycle used are on board and active! If all goes as planned, completing the part of the Work Cycle associated with the Execution stage becomes a straightforward "build it," "assemble it," or "make it."

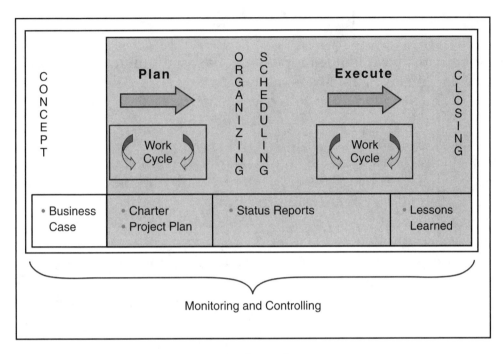

Figure 4.2 Project Management Life Cycle. © Copyright 2007 Pamela McGhee and Peter McAliney.

Work that was planned is performed and there is a change control mechanism in place to incorporate the inevitable changes that will arise during the course of the Work Cycle. Don't forget, changes also take place in Planning and are governed by the change control mechanism as well.

Delivering the product or service to the owners (stakeholders, sponsor, clients, users) is the next to the last step of the project. The last stop on the road map is the Project Close or Project Post Mortem, the capturing of what worked well (and worked not so well), the completion of project documentation, the closing of the financial and administrative books, the reassignment of project team members, and the addition of the project files to the organization's project history database for future reference. (Those who do not study history are condemned to repeat it.)

Validating the Business Case

You have just been handed a Business Case with multiple notebooks, meeting minutes, flip charts, and electronic files. The project manager is now ready to jump into developing the project plan, or is she? Not so fast, there are some things to do first.

As project manager, your first duty is to exercise due diligence and review the Business Case. Make certain that you understand what the investigator developed with the business sponsor and stakeholders (if you were the investigator, this is a very short exercise). In reality, the Business Case is often not as cleanly developed as we painted in Chapter 3. You may get a partial Business Case—or none at all. You may be told to "just do it!" In any event, the project manager needs to make certain that there is a solid Business Case from which he or she can develop a project plan. Validating the Business Case *must* occur before you begin the next step.

A project manager is typically appointed at the start of the Work Cycle, or as soon as the Business Case has been approved, while the sponsor and stakeholders may have been working the project from the start of the Business Case. As the newly appointed project manager, you need to be very sensitive to the work that these players have done. You need to establish trust and provide them with the confidence that you are the right person for the job.

TIP

If you are appointed project manager on a team with a sponsor and stakeholders who developed the Business Case, take the time—make the time—at the beginning of your tenure to get to know your team. Ask questions and listen, listen, listen.

Forming the Team

The success of the project lies very much in the team that will deliver the goods. You know you are off to a good start—after all, you are the project manager. Sometimes you get to pick your team—other times you do not. The business sponsor is a given (that's who appointed you in the first place). The stakeholders also come with the project. But what about the team?

To the extent that you have any input, you want to create a balanced team. Look for individuals in the organization that have complementary talents. A combination of seasoned veterans and young up-and-comers is an ideal mix. You will learn even at this early stage in the project, that negotiating is an all-important project management skill. Some of your team members will be foisted upon you, but to the extent you are able, make a strong case for getting one or two solid team members who you know you will be able to count on to make the project a success.

At the beginning of this stage, the project manager, the sponsor, and stakeholders need to clearly establish roles, responsibilities, and communication protocols. Establish early on who is doing what, at what point during the project communications need to occur, and other details about the project (see Figure 4.3). While developing the Business Case, lack of clarity was acceptable (and necessary), clarity will be of utmost importance as the project begins to unfold.

You will find out one of the overriding duties of a project manager is managing expectations—both up and down in the organization.

Planning the Work

Your goal in the Planning stage is to develop a Project Charter and a Project Plan (see Figure 4.1 on p. 58). These two deliverables will

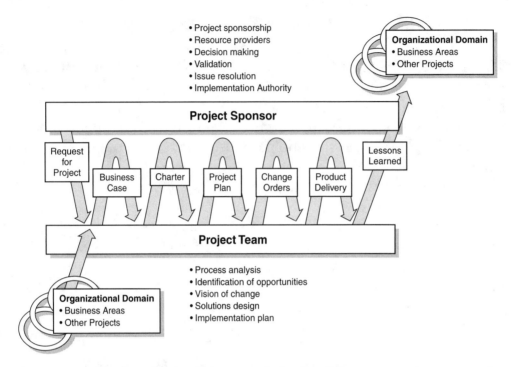

Figure 4.3   Sponsor-Project Manager Relationship. © Copyright 2007 Pamela McGhee and Peter McAliney.

form the IPP—the road map that you will present to the project sponsor for approval (see Figure 4.4).

How do we start this journey? With the Planning—the largest piece.

Let's go back to our road map from Chapter 1, with an addition (the IPP).

The end result of Planning is an IPP. The first component of the IPP is that all-important Project Charter (see Table 4.1 on p. 64).

The project manager's first action in Planning is to develop, with the sponsor and major stakeholders, the Project Charter—the steering wheel for the entire project. Its importance cannot be over emphasized. As the project manager, you are responsible for seeing that it is developed and developed accurately, according to sponsor and stakeholder objectives. The project will only be as good as its Charter.

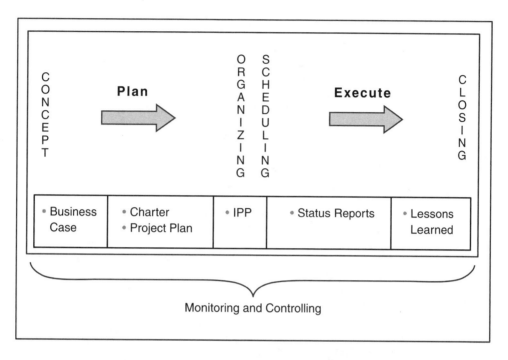

Figure 4.4 The Enhanced PMLC Shell—The Road Map with the Integrated Project Plan (IPP). © Copyright 2007 Pamela McGhee and Peter McAliney.

The Project Charter

Good news—the Business Case and the Project Charter overlap. If a good Business Case document is created, the Project Charter is already half written. The Charter should have a number of "must have" elements (see Table 4.2).

It's important to remember as you are developing the Charter, you will be working in iterations. Draft after draft will be reviewed and reviewed. We can only hope—reviews and responses mean sponsor and stakeholder commitment to the project—a key element in project success.

Table 4.1   The Integrated Project Plan
(Short Version)

Project Charter (Statement of Scope or Project Scope Document)
- Risk identification
- Assumptions
- Constraints
- Primary project driver
- List of stakeholders

Work Breakdown Structure (WBS) to the Task Level
- Risk planning/mitigation

Logic Diagram
- Network
- Event/precedence

Gantt Chart
- Schedule (Time and labor costs)

Cost Spreadsheet (Nonlabor Costs Associated with Tasks)

© Copyright 2007 Pamela McGhee and Peter McAliney.

TIP

At certain intervals, the project manager will want to circulate an iteration (the current draft) to the sponsor and relevant stakeholders for comments and reactions. (How often or even if, is dependent on the culture of the organization—its management style.) The really savvy project manager will also circulate the draft to those lower in the chain of command who really know and work in the business areas within the scope of the project. She will want those on the front lines to know what management is "cooking up." This will save mistakes in refining those requirements later on.

However, politics here can be rampant, strong, and lethal. Watch out! While we suggest circulating a draft to selected SMEs for a reality check, first find out if this is politically acceptable in your organization. In some organizational cultures this is common practice. In others, it's verboten. Find out before circulating.

Table 4.2   Project Charter Template

Project Charter: Sample Outline for Smaller Projects

Project Mission Statement

- Articulated link to corporate mission statement
- Articulated link to division mission statement

Project Goal Statement

Statement of Scope (can include a visualization)

Project Objectives

Critical Success Factors

Critical Success Measures

List of Relevant Risks

List of Assumptions

Project Constraints

Primary Project Driver

Identification of All

- Stakeholders
- Sponsors
- Clients
- Other interested parties

Every time you move forward, you will constantly be looking back to earlier definitions; Goals, Scope, Objectives, Critical Success Factors, Critical Success Measures (which are actually high level requirements), Risks, Constraints, and other components to increase the precision of both your thinking and the thinking of the sponsor and stakeholders. The later iterations of the Charter will be far more accurate than the earlier iterations, leading to more accurate estimates later on in Planning.

Next, we will develop and present in stages (the Project Charter will "unfold," element by element) the development of a Project Charter for a project at the "We See It Better Company" using our Project Charter template (Table 4.2).

Project Mission Statement

Start by working with the project sponsor and stakeholders by revisiting the Project Mission Statement that you developed in the Concept stage. As we discussed, the Mission Statement encapsulates the final purpose of the project. The Project Mission Statement should be aligned with the corporate or organizational Mission Statement *and* the departmental or divisional Mission Statement. It should be related to both as a subcategory.

Following our mantra of strategic alignment, we start with the corporate Vision Statement at the top of the strategic plan document (see Table 4.3).

With the Strategic Plan as a starting point, the company can start to map out projects. There are four strategic goals, each having one or more strategic objectives. Of course, all goals cannot be satisfied by one project. To satisfy the strategic goals listed will require many projects as well as a good deal of functional (nonproject) work.

We'll separate out one project stemming from corporate strategic goal D, strategic objective D2, "Develop a viable Internet market that will bring in significant sales revenue."

We'll name the project "Buy See It Better Online."

Ideally, the project sponsor and major stakeholders should formulate the Project Mission Statement, which should be business-oriented, arising from the business environment or reference frame. The Project Mission Statement answers the question of *what* we are going to do (Table 4.4).

Table 4.3   Strategic Plan Document

Confidential: Not to Be Distributed outside of the
***We See It Better* Company**

Strategic Plan Document
D-R-A-F-T
The *We See It Better* Company

Our Vision

We extend your vision for the present and the future.

Our Mission

To become the premiere provider of high-powered, computer-assisted visual devices for all consumer, government, and military markets.

Our Strategic Goals

Goal A: Become a supplier of computer-assisted visual devices to the U.S. Military.

Objectives:

A1 Provide unique, nonaggressive, state-of-the-art visual technologies.
A2 Provide technology that cannot be easily converted to offensive weapons.
A3 Provide technology that will help save the lives of soldiers.

Goal B: Become a supplier of computer-assisted visual devices to the U.S. Government.

Objectives:

B1 Develop prototypes of cost-effective, computer-assisted visual devices for use in governmental areas such as national parks, wildlife preserves, reservoirs, airports, and so on.
B2 Identify and/or create a market for this product category.
B3 Obtain some level of government funding via a "product development partnership."

Goal C: Diversify and expand our consumer market.

Objective:

Develop markets for our consumer products in Asia, the Middle East, Africa, and Europe.

Goal D: Sell our products over the Internet while maintaining our traditional retail base.

Objectives:

D1 Achieve a sound Internet presence and visibility.
D2 Develop a viable Internet market that will bring in significant sales revenue.
D3 Ensure the Internet market will not compete with our traditional retail base.

Table 4.4   Project Mission Statement

Project name	Buy *We See It Better* Online
Code name	Busy Bee DD2
Project Mission Statement	To create and expand a worldwide Internet buying platform with name recognition, pizzazz, ease of access and use, and a tech-savvy feel that adds up to "Buy Me, Now!"

From Corporate Strategic Goal D, Objective D2. © Copyright 2007 Pamela McGhee and Peter McAliney.

Project Goal Statement

The Project Goal statement answers the question of *how* we are going to accomplish the mission. We may have one mission, but there can be many *hows* to accomplish it. We have noticed that stakeholders often confuse the mission (*what*) with the *how*. Some *hows* are less expensive than others, some are easier than others. As project manager, it is your job to set them straight.

TIP

People always find it easier to jump to the *how* before the *what* is fully fleshed out. As project manager, you cannot let this happen. Make sure the *what* has been answered, makes sense, and is communicated before you let the *how* conversation occur.

The example shown in Table 4.5 shows the important distinction between the project mission and the project goal(s). A project may have multiple goals.

Statement of Scope

A good Business Case will contain 80 percent of the project's scope. It's a matter of revisiting the completed Needs and Wants template

Table 4.5   Project Goal Statement

Project name	Buy *We See It Better* Online
Code name	Busy Bee DD2
Project Goals	D2.1 Customers, present and future, will know something great is coming.
	D2.2 A quirky, attention-grabbing web site will illustrate products that you can almost touch.
	D2.3 An easy, secure purchasing mechanism that uses any currency or payment instrument will be provided.
	D2.4 Customers will come back to our site or go to a retail outlet to buy more *We See It Better* products.

From Project Mission Statement and Corporate Strategic Goal D, Objective D2. © Copyright 2007 Pamela McGhee and Peter McAliney.

(see Table 3.1 on p. 35). As we discussed before, however, you will want to conduct a due diligence on what was created in the Business Case. Go back and talk to the project sponsor and stakeholders and discuss their original input. Because the time to actually do the work is now closer, and as a project team, you have more information to inform the conversation with the project sponsor and stakeholders, you will be able to get better clarity around the needs and wants that were articulated weeks (or even months) ago.

The smaller the project scope, the more likely the project is to be successful. In addition, the shorter the time lapse between freezing the project specifications and delivering the product, the more likely the project is to be successful—both augur well for spending that time in planning. Table 4.6 illustrates the project scope for our example of the "We See It Better Company" project.

Project Objectives

Project objectives can be tricky. In part, it is because they must be determined by the stakeholders, and also because the many stakeholders must agree on them. For practical purposes, the project manager

Table 4.6   Project Scope Statement

Project name	Buy *We See It Better* Online
Code name	Busy Bee DD2
Statement of Scope	This project will encompass marketing (print and electronic media), Web and computer technology, required financial functions, and client creation and retention practices.
(may include a visualization)	

From Project Mission Statement and Corporate Strategic Goal D, Objective D2. © Copyright 2007 Pamela McGhee and Peter McAliney.

must attempt to keep the number of objectives down to a reasonable number—say four to seven, at the most. If the number of demanded objectives climbs exponentially, you probably have a number of projects on your hands, not just one. Note how the objectives for our sample project add further clarity and manage expectations for the specified project (see Table 4.7).

Critical Success Factors (CSFs)

After developing those project objectives, we can start developing Critical Success Factors (CSFs) that are qualitative criteria which, if

Table 4.7   Project Objectives

Project name	Buy *We See It Better* Online
Code name	Busy Bee DD2
Project Objectives	We will use Critical Success Factors (defined as Objectives):
	D2.3.1 Online purchasing is not time consuming.
	D2.3.2 Online purchasing has flexible payment methods.
	D2.3.3 Online purchasing must be usable by the non-technology-savvy client.
	D.2.3.4 Users must know that their funds are safe.
	D.2.3.5 Language cannot be a barrier.

From Project Goal D2.3 An easy, secure purchasing mechanism that uses any currency or payment instrument will be provided. © Copyright 2007 Pamela McGhee and Peter McAliney.

met, will prove that the project produced a successful product or service. There are two ways to write project objectives. Project objectives may bear a one-to-one relationship to the CSFs, or one project objective may give rise to several CSFs. Mid-level client management best generates these factors.

In Table 4.7, one project objective *is* a CSF.

Critical Success Measures (CSMs)

Next, we work with stakeholders to generate the Critical Success Measures (CSMs) for the project. These are best generated by mid- to lower-level client management. Critical Success Measures are *quantitative* (numeric, metrics) and may be viewed as high-level requirements. For each CSF there may be more than one CSM, but there must be at least one (see Table 4.8).

TIP

As project manager, you need to make certain that you do not have too many—or conflicting—CSMs.

Table 4.8　Critical Success Measures

Project name	Buy *We See It Better* Online
Code name	Busy Bee DD2
Critical Success Measures	D.2.3.1 Transactions will be processed within 10 seconds unless the buyer causes a delay.
	D.2.3.2 Customers may change their minds on method of payment midtransaction, without having to re-enter all of their data.
	D.2.3.3 Customers can get help when they ask for it.
	D.2.3.4 The system will meet international standards for secure funds transfer.
	D.2.3.5 All major world languages will be available upon request.

Table 4.9   Project Risks

Project name	Buy *We See It Better* Online
Code name	Busy Bee DD2
List of Relevant Risks	DD2.R1 Business: The costs of developing a worldwide buying platform will outstrip expected revenues.
	DD2.R2 Technical: Technology infrastructure in some nations may not support security, and/or other features.
	DD2.R3 Organizational: We may lack understanding of financial patterns and buying behavior of overseas clients
	DD2.R4 Geopolitical: Possible local government intervention and/or restrictions.

Relevant Risks

Risk means uncertainty and uncertainty can have a positive or negative outcome. Risks are unknowns. It is incumbent on the sponsor, stakeholders, clients, the project manager, and the project team to identify as many risks as possible (business, technical, organization, political, etc.) as early on in the project as possible. Risk identification is ongoing. As more and more becomes known about the project, additional risks may be identified while identified risks may fade into oblivion.

Table 4.9 shows some identified risks for the "We See It Better Company" project, "Buy See It Better Online."

Assumptions

Assumptions allow us to extend (and extrapolate) the knowledge base of the project. There are technical and scientific assumptions, administrative and organizational assumptions, asset and resource availability assumptions, as well as macro-level assumptions that are so global and pervasive that they must be acknowledged and cannot be negotiated away.

Table 4.10   Project Assumptions

Project name	Buy *We See It Better* Online
Code name	Busy Bee DD2
List of Assumptions	DD2.A1 Business: Project funding has been established and is available.
	DD2.A2 Technical: Hardware and software to meet project needs exist in the marketplace.
	DD2.A3 Organizational: Parts of the project may be out-sourced.
	DD2.A4 Geopolitical: Access to some Internet content will be restricted in some nations.
	DD2.A5 Profound: Cultural practices in some world regions may affect design and products offered.

The project sponsor and stakeholders have assumptions, as do the project manager and the project team. It is important to get them all out and down on paper where they can be seen and examined.

Curiously, assumptions are often the flip side of risks and whether a particular item is listed as an assumption or as a risk can be a matter of style.

The project assumptions for our "Buy See It Better Online" project are listed in Table 4.10.

Project Constraints

Constraints narrow the project manager's range of options available to plan, schedule, execute, and control the project. Constraints can fall into business, financial, administrative, organizational, legal, and other categories.

All projects are beset by constraints. It is best to identify them explicitly, as early as possible, and place them in the Project Charter. In Table 4.11, we show a few constraints restricting our project.

Table 4.11   Project Constraints

Project name	Buy *We See It Better* Online
Code name	Busy Bee DD2
List of Constraints	DD2.C1 Business: The budget ceiling on this project is $2 million.
	DD2.C2 Technical: Any acquired hardware/software must be maintainable in house.
	DD2.C3 Organizational: Existing phone-order staff must also handle Internet orders. No additional staff will be added.
	DD2.C4 Business: Time to market must not exceed one year.

Primary Project Driver

Remember Figure 2.5 on page 23 depicting the project manager's universe? Well, it's back as Figure 4.5!

One of the three sides of that triangle will be the primary driver of the project. The project manager makes project decisions to preserve that driver's dominance. If time is the project driver, then all will be sacrificed to schedule. If scope/requirements is the driver,

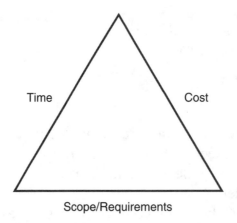

Figure 4.5   The Project Management Triangle. © Copyright 2007 Pamela McGhee and Peter McAliney.

Table 4.12   Project Primary Driver

Project name	Buy *We See It Better* Online
Code name	Busy Bee DD2
Primary Project Driver	Cost
Secondary Project Driver	Scope/requirements (ease of use)

then late delivery and over budget situations will be tolerated. If cost is the driver, then lateness and scope/requirements deficits will be tolerated.

Who determines the primary driver? The sponsor and major stakeholders do. To further complicate the situation, there can be a secondary driver, forcing the project manager into gravity defying acrobatics (see our book's cover). Table 4.12 contains our project driver statement.

Project Stakeholders, Sponsor, Clients, and Other Interested Parties

It is important to know who all of the players in the project are. The savvy project manager compiles a complete cast of characters and lists them in a playbill (Table 4.13). Distribute the cast list, noting what role each plays in the project.

TIP

All projects will have naysayers. Whether you list the negative stakeholders in the Project Charter is a matter of political acumen and judgment. In any case, list all stakeholders, from high to low.

Table 4.13   Project Stakeholders, Sponsors, Clients, and Other Interested Parties

Project name	Buy *We See It Better* Online
Code name	Busy Bee DD2
Stakeholders	All regional managers, Marketing
	All regional managers, Product Development
	All customer service managers
Sponsors	Executive Vice President, International Marketing
	Executive Vice President, Consumer Product Development
Clients	Customer service staff
Interested parties	Military product line
	Governmental product line
	Retail stores

Project Charter Sign-Offs

Obtaining Project Charter sign-offs from the project's sponsor and major stakeholders may require developing many iterations and revisions of the Charter. Remember, all involved must agree on the goals, objectives, deliverables, and so on. This may take a while. It's not unusual for the Project Charter to continue to evolve for a significant period of time during planning. Like diplomatic negotiations, agreement and compromise take time. A good rule of thumb is to push (demand) Charter sign off by the time that one-third of the planning time has elapsed. If major stakeholders and the sponsor have not been able to come to agreement and commitment by then, there is probably a significant problem in the structure of the project (too large a scope?), in the usefulness of the defined deliverables (unclear or conflicting objectives), or any number of undefined issues, including political ones.

However, the competent project manager does not wait until the Charter is signed by all. When the Charter is reasonably solid, the project manager and the project team launch headlong into the next step in Planning, the "as is" analysis.

The detailed road map in Figure 4.6 shows the way.

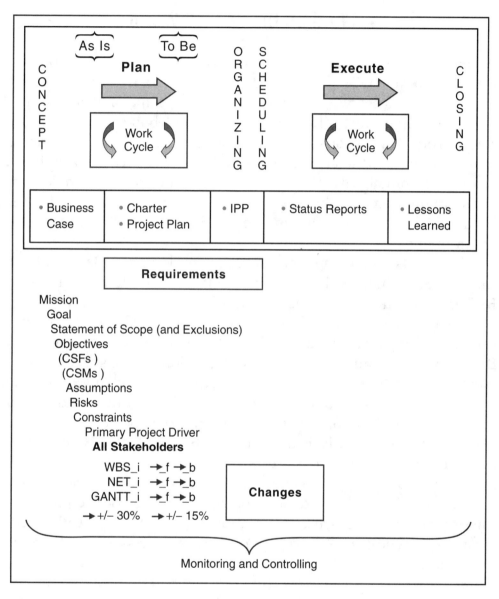

Figure 4.6 The Planning Road Map. © Copyright 2007 Pamela McGhee and Peter McAliney.

A Word on the "As Is" World

Why assess and document the "As Is"? Because it is the environment with which you will work to produce the "To Be"—the product/ service the project will produce. You may think of it as the real baseline of the work effort. In addition, although you have just been through a rigorous Charter definition, spending time and resources to assess the current environment will further familiarize project personnel with the project real estate, politics, major and not-so-major players, business processes and practices, as well as allowing time for the informal emergence of reality-based requirements.

The "As Is" is a component of scope development. Because scope can also be defined as the difference between the "As Is" and the "To Be," understanding the "As Is" will assist in scope verification.

There are a number of Work Cycle related tools and techniques used to develop an accurate "As Is" picture. Interviews, observation, Data Flow Diagrams, Process Flows, questionnaires, surveys, documentation reading, and the most effective of all—going and living with the clients/stakeholders for a while, while watching and recording everything they do, are techniques and tools borrowed from the Business Systems Analysis and Design (BSA&D) Work Cycle. However, effectiveness will cost resources (read that as money). How much are you (really, the sponsor) willing to spend on the quintessential "As Is"? This will depend on the criticality of the project. A mission-critical, high-risk, high-impact project may well justify such an expenditure of project resources. A less critical project might not.

Regardless, for each project, the competent project manager takes at least a decent swipe at the "As Is." As we have said, it is the basis for the "To Be"—the product/service to be produced by the project you have been selected to manage. Neglect the "As Is" at your peril.

What's Next?

Remember that Charter and those CSMs as high-level requirements? Now, it's time to get serious. Either verify and refine those requirements, revise them (you may have gotten the wrong end of the stick in the Charter—or perhaps the right people were not involved in developing the Charter in the first place) or go back to the drawing board and reassess the validity of that Charter. (Yes, at times during the planning activities after the Charter, we find that the Charter needs significant revision.)

The project could die at this point, just as it could have been terminated at the Business Case. But, if not, we proceed to the requirements analysis.

Requirements Analysis

Even though the project manager and the project team are immersed in requirements analysis, both need to start thinking about developing the WBS before getting too far into refining those requirements. This means that you'll be developing several renditions of the WBS, changing it as you begin to understand and further refine the final requirements. Welcome to project management, but to be forewarned is to be forearmed.

Just how do you analyze and refine requirements?

Remember to use the Project Charter as a touchstone while you are gathering and analyzing requirements. Any requirements that emerge that are not covered in the Charter must be analyzed as to whether they are within scope. Again, do not be surprised if the Charter needs to be revised. Of course, this will necessitate another round of approvals and sign-offs—but that's the nature of the job—and projects.

Developing a separate Requirements Document to append to the Charter is proper and due diligence. That document should also go through a round of stakeholder sign-offs. Do not drown your stakeholders in too much detail, however. Provide an Executive Abstract at the front end, summarizing, at a higher level, the contents of the Requirements Document.

Here is a checklist for efficient requirements analysis:

- Document how the environment within the project scope works today ("As Is").
- Define the general business requirements—what the product or service produced by the project must provide for the sponsor, stakeholders, and any and all product or service users.
- Develop the actual requirements *with* the stakeholders:
  —Hold timed meetings (about 45 minutes) with a focused agenda. Hold as many of them as necessary, grouping stakeholders by level, category, and occasionally mix levels and categories so that stakeholders are aware of mutual and exclusive requirements. Have a flip chart scribe and a note taker in attendance. Have the meeting results written up and distributed to all stakeholders.
  —Hold as many meetings as needed for complete definition.
- Define and document how the environment and product/service should work in the future ("To Be.")
- Produce a Requirements Document and obtain sign-offs from the relevant parties. (Remember, there may be multiple iterations.)
- Do not forget that the most important part of the Requirements Document is the Executive Abstract. (It is all that many will read.) Make it short and accurate. Use business English, not Work Cycle-related technical language.

In the requirements analysis process, make certain that the role of the project manager is well defined. Is he or she assisting in the definition of business requirements, or technical requirements, or both?

Now, for the WBS, the quintessential statement of project scope and the realization of *all* work that must be done to produce the product or service the project was formed to create.

The Work Breakdown Structure

Remember that shortly after the requirements analysis process, you prudently started to develop the WBS? Well, get ready to develop the most important component of the project plan, the heart of the project plan—the WBS.

TIP

The **WBS** is the final, the quintessential statement of project scope. If it's not in the **WBS**, you will not be able to build it, cost it, or schedule it and it won't be a part of the final product. (Unless you go over budget, come in late, and drive your project team members, and yourself, bananas—not to mention getting bad reviews for poor performance!)

Developing a Work Breakdown Structure

When projects are first evaluated and selected, they are largely defined by a vision of goals, strategies, and deliverables. But once the go-ahead is given, this vision must be quickly translated into a series of tangible tasks (work components) that can be executed and completed by the project team.

The WBS defines the work that must be done to create the product or service the project was created to produce.

Within standardized project management practices, the specification of project tasks is referred to as a WBS. The WBS is an essential project planning component, serving as the foundation (heart) of the project plan.

Here is the PMLC tool progression:

Project Charter → WBS → Network → Gantt → Cost Spreadsheet

Depending on project needs and technical capabilities, the WBS can be produced as a simple list, as a detailed report, or in graphical format, but the goal of any WBS is clear: to translate project goals, deliverables, and processes into a structured picture of tangible work components. The WBS provides a road map for the project team, laying out the overall work effort required.

There is no single approach to WBS preparation, nor is there one format to follow. WBS complexity and detail vary based on project needs, available technical tools, and the level of experience with the type of project on hand. Regardless of complexity and format, WBS preparation is simplified when a standardized, structured approach is taken. To facilitate the process, you can take a "building block" approach.

In Chapter 2, we introduced the Work Cycle, representing the way the work is done to produce the product or service the project was formulated to create.

The Work Cycle is back! Curiously, using the Work Cycle (phases) is one of the ways to organize the WBS (see Figure 4.7).

In the building block approach, we can use one or more of several techniques. A WBS can be organized by Work Cycle.

By Work Cycle, we mean the order or sequence of the work done to produce the product or service. For example, when creating a business system, first we do the analysis, then the design, then the development, so the corresponding Work Cycle would be Analysis . . . Design . . . Development. These elements could constitute the top layer of the WBS. We would then break each element into its lower-level components.

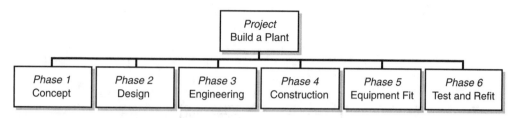

Figure 4.7   A WBS Can Be Organized by Work Cycle. © Copyright 2007 Pamela McGhee and Peter McAliney.

Another method is organizing by subject matter or content. If the purpose of our project is to produce a banquet, we can pose the question "Of what does a banquet consist?" Well, for one thing, food. Then there is furniture (people have to sit somewhere and put their dinner plates somewhere else). Banquets have guest speakers. That is another category, and there are many more (see Figure 4.8). One method of **WBS** organization is not necessarily superior to another. At times, the product or service to be produced will lend itself more easily to one technique or another.

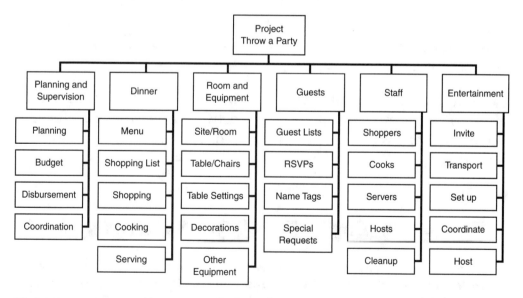

Figure 4.8   A WBS Can Be Organized by Content or Subject Matter.
© Copyright 2007 Pamela McGhee and Peter McAliney.

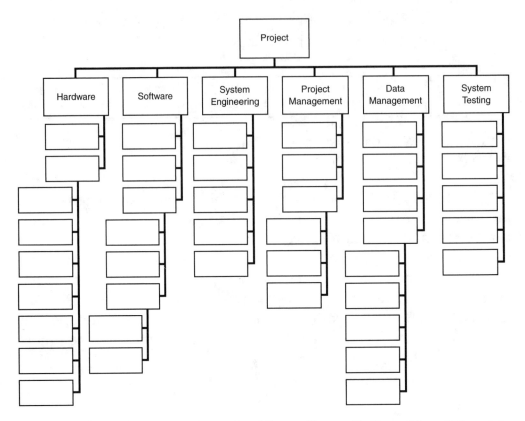

Figure 4.9   A WBS Can Be Organized According to Deliverables. © Copyright 2007 Pamela McGhee and Peter McAliney.

A third technique of WBS organization is by deliverables (Figure 4.9). Determine what must be delivered as final results and make those deliverables the top layer of the WBS and decompose from there.

TIP

We have found that when we know a lot about the subject matter, Work Cycle WBS organization works well. It also fits easily when the "building" is essentially linear. Content or subject matter WBS organization works well when there are many threads that do not necessarily interact with each other but all threads must reach the same end point. Frankly, when we do not have a clue, the first approach we take is deliverables—here's what we have to deliver—now let's figure out how to make it.

Your WBS building plan should begin as a sketch—a rough outline of the work required to complete your project. As you and your team sit down to create this sketch, you must be prepared to answer the following questions:

- What work must be done to achieve project results?
- How much effort time is required to complete each task?
- How will the work be structured (level of granularity—the size of the lowest level task)?

The WBS presents a hierarchical view of a project. As you begin WBS preparation, you will need to look at your project from multiple levels, starting at the highest level, digging down to details, and fitting in your various "building blocks" along the way.

Below are examples of WBS hierarchy and numbering schema:

- Task Declension
- Granularity to the fourth level
- Alternate terminologies (Figure 4.10)

To what level of detail (aka granularity) should a WBS descend (Table 4.14)? The answer is: It depends!

What is the level of experience of the project workers? The more expert the workers, the less granularity you will probably need. Also to be factored in are the risks and impacts of the project. Even if you have expert team members, mission-critical projects need to be planned (greater WBS granularity) to the nth degree.

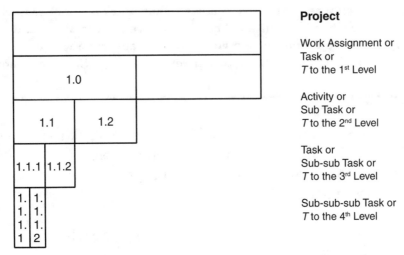

Figure 4.10   A Leveled WBS. © Copyright 2007 Pamela McGhee and
Peter McAliney.

Using the WBS as the First Step in Developing Estimates

Directions: Start by representing your project as the top rectangle labeled "Project." If the amount of work to be done is greater than 20 hours of effort for the average qualified professional (nose to keyboard—no break, lunch, bathroom, or sleep time—the amount of time the work would take if you sat down and never got up until the work was finished), then divide that top rectangle into pieces (Work Assignments). If each of those Work Assignments is over 20 hours of effort, then divide those Work Assignments into smaller Activities. If each of those Activities is greater than 20 hours of effort, divide those Activities into smaller Tasks, and so on and so on until the lowest level work components are around 20 hours (a reasonable range is 3.5 hours to a high of around 28 hours) of effort for the average qualified professional.

Why have we chosen the "magic" number of 20 hours? Because it amounts to about a calendar week's worth of work. Using a divisor of 20 hours gives us weekly control. Each week, the project manager can look at status, actual versus planned, and get a fairly accurate reading of whether the project is on schedule and within budget.

Table 4.14   Work Breakdown Structure Example

Your goal: Quantify the work effort required to build your new file server.

What level of detail best suits this goal?

Less control over project work
  1.1 Inventory hardware and software
  1.2 Configure hardware
  1.3 Install software

OR

More control over project work
  1.1   Inventory hardware and software
  1.1.1 Open boxes
  1.1.2 Unpack hardware
  1.1.3 Unpack software
  1.1.4 Complete inventory

© Copyright 2007 Pamela McGhee and Peter McAliney.

TIP

The granularity of the WBS we develop during Planning determines our future control over the project during Execution.

If we had chosen a 40-hour divisor to granularize (drill down) the WBS, then actual versus planned measurements would have been possible every two weeks. WBS granularity (lower-level details) and effort estimates lead us to the next problem.

How do we estimate effort if the work is new work and we have no historical knowledge of how long the work *should* take?

There is a formula:

$$\text{Task effort} = \frac{4 \times \begin{pmatrix} \text{Most Likely} \\ \text{estimate} \end{pmatrix} + \begin{pmatrix} \text{Most Optimistic} \\ \text{estimate} \end{pmatrix} + \begin{pmatrix} \text{Most Pessimistic} \\ \text{estimate} \end{pmatrix}}{6}$$

However, this does not help if you don't know the work in the first place!

Good news! There is a way of estimating Task size in a WBS when the project manager and the project team are not sufficiently knowledgeable about the work.

How? Call the experts in that work. Describe your work components. Get several opinions of most likely, optimistic, and pessimistic estimates. Average each category, and then apply the formula. While no guarantee of success, it's better than sticking your finger in the air to see which way the wind is blowing.

By the way, the name attached to this formula is PERT (Program Evaluation and Review Technique—from the U.S. Navy—not to be confused with PERT Chart, which is the older term for a network.)

Very briefly, applying this formula gives an outcome based on a Beta curve or distribution (skewed to the right), or the most *likely* outcome, statistically speaking. See our Appendix if you'd like a more detailed explanation.

In developing a WBS for the product or service to be delivered, the best and most accurate approach is to have the project team construct the WBS with the (limited) participation of the project manager. Of course, if you are resource poor, the project manager pitches in with the rest of the team to build what may be at first a high level WBS.

The smaller the lowest level tasks, in effort hours, the more accurate your estimates are likely to be (like estimating the number of jelly beans in a small glass versus estimating the number of jelly beans in a large fish tank). There is a catch, however: to granularize (drill down) to very small tasks, the smaller the lowest level tasks, the more oversight and measuring the project manager must do, and the more hours the project manager must put in to manage the project.

This extended overhead may be warranted for mission-critical, high-risk, high-impact projects, but may not be cost or resource effective for projects that are not as critical (Figure 3.3 on p. 39). Table 4.15 will help you visualize this.

Table 4.15   Work Breakdown Structure

Project							
Work Assignment				Work Assignment (Large task)			
Activity		Activity		Activity		Activity	
Task	Task	Task	Task	Task	Task	Task	(Small task)

© Copyright 2007 Pamela McGhee and Peter McAliney.

TIP

A project manager may be able to simultaneously manage three or so low-risk, low-impact projects relatively easily, but will be severely pushed (overtime and agitation) with one project in the high-risk, high-impact category.

The larger the task or work component used, the less control the project manager has over the project because measuring actual to plan progress occurs less frequently and because the work components (tasks) are large and are more difficult to estimate, effort-wise, than smaller, more easily realized components with fewer unrecognized interdependencies.

To summarize, the larger the task size, the less likely the estimate is to be realistic and accurate. The trade-off is that the project manager does not have to spend as much time managing the project.

TIP

The competent project manager may be able to manage several smaller projects of large granularity, but will most likely have to work overtime to manage one larger project of fine granularity.

The Logic Diagram (Network, Precedence, PERT Chart)

Dependency Analysis

Using the WBS, the effective project manager (the person who delegates) has the project team sequence the tasks at the lowest level of each leg of the WBS in the logical order that the tasks must be worked on and completed in order to develop the product or service. This will be the logic diagram, or network, which is the basis of a project schedule.

As with the WBS, the entire core project team will need to participate in the creation of the logic diagram. Many heads are better than one (the Gestalt effect).

Don't forget to include the effort estimates from the WBS along with the task name. Determine the length of each path. The longest path will be the critical path, which represents the shortest amount of time in which the work can be done, relative to dependencies.

You and your team will repeat this sequencing many times, as you develop detailed requirements for the product and learn more about the work that must *really* be done to deliver the right results to the stakeholders and clients. Do not be surprised at going through these iterations more than a dozen times or so.

You are now well on your way to determining a schedule, in calendar days, for the work to be done.

Here's a simple logic diagram with a critical path of 16 effort units (see Figure 4.11). An effort unit can be defined as any time unit desired. Most frequently, that unit is hours. However, it can be days or any other desired time unit. (We do *recommend* hours.)

The task name from the WBS is above the line and the effort length, below. This type of network is called *task on line*. We add up the length of each path. The *longest* path is the critical path, representing the shortest amount of time in which the work can be done, relative to dependencies.

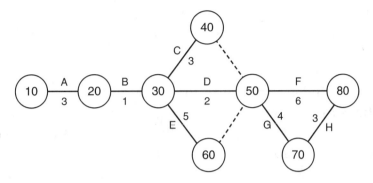

Figure 4.11 Network Diagram. © Copyright 2007 Pamela McGhee and Peter McAliney.

Path A, B, C, F has a length of 13 effort units. The middle path, A, B, D, F has a length of 12 effort units. The lower path, A, B, E, G, H has a length of 16 effort units and therefore is the critical path. Simply put, the work represented by this network cannot be completed in less than 16 effort units relative to dependencies.

If we use days instead of effort units, the critical path is 16 days of effort long. The work represented by the network cannot be completed in less than 16 days of effort, relative to dependencies.

Float

You have noted that in Figure 4.11, the critical path is 16 effort units long. The other, non-critical paths are shorter by 3 and 4 effort units, respectively. The amount by which they are shorter is defined as *float*. In our example, task C, while 3 effort units in length can dally around for 2 units without jeopardizing the project. However, if C dallies for more than 2 units, the critical path moves from E to C and the project will be late unless some other adjustment is made. The length of the path including C was 13 units. There were 3 units to spare. If C dallied for more than 2 units, the length of that path segment increases to above 5. This causes the critical path to jump to C, and then continue along to G and H. So now the critical path is A(3), plus B(1), plus C(5+), plus G(4), plus H(3); which when added equal 16+.

Float may indeed give dallying time, but once that float is exceeded, the project may be late.

On a more serious note, that dallying time gives the project manager leeway and options. Suppose Carol was assigned to do task C and Eric to do task E. Early in E, Eric approaches the project manager, "I am in trouble, I won't finish on time—Help!" If Carol has the skills to help Eric with E, the project manager can transfer Carol to E for a maximum of 2 effort units. Carol is successful in getting Eric and E back on schedule in 2 or less than 2 effort units. Wonderful!

But even though you, as project manager, have saved the delivery date, you have increased the cost of the project.

In project costing, costs are accrued by task. If a task in the WBS is executed, its cost is applied to the project. In the baseline project plan, task E was costed as consisting of the labor of Eric. When Carol was added, her costs were also applied to E, thus, departing from the baseline budget plan. E although completed on time, cost more (Carol plus Eric) than planned, resulting in an increased project budget.

Note that in the case, above, the project manager got off cheaply! Carol, already on the project, could pitch in. What if no employee was available? Well, then the project manager might have to resort to a "rent-a-body" (otherwise known as a Consultant), resulting in a much larger cost to the project!

Lateness always costs!

Remember that!

As with the WBS, the project team will go through a number of iterations of the network. If the WBS is changed (tasks added or deleted), then the changed WBS must be resequenced, and a new network created, which very possibly has a different critical path. Be prepared to go through any number of iterations. Remember, our desired outcome is an accurate project schedule.

The Gantt Chart

Every couple of iterations, the project manager and team will want to turn that network into a Gantt Chart or project schedule to see what is being produced, schedule-wise. How do we convert from our logic network (in effort) to a realistic calendar schedule (in duration)?

The Elephant in the Living Room

We may indeed work a 40-hour week, but we are not productive (doing actual nose to keyboard work) for those entire 40 hours. First, there is lunch. Subtract 5 hours from that 40. Of the 35 hours left, 7.5 are for maintenance; coffee, bathroom, routine office interaction, and other events. This leaves the well-disciplined worker with 27.5 hours per business week left for actual work. If we are dedicated full time to one project task, it will take us almost one week to complete that task. Therefore, one 20-hour task will take almost one calendar week on our Gantt Chart, if the project worker is scheduled full time on that task. If he or she can devote only four hours per week to that task, the time span (duration) for that task will stretch out to 5 weeks on the Gantt Chart. In this situation, the manager lending that worker takes all of the hits re: lunch and bathroom, and so on. If that lending manager lends the worker half time, then the project manager and the lending (functional manager) share the productivity hit 50/50 (6.25 hours each).

Realistically, the project is charged the cost of 40 hours (worker's "salary" plus overhead) for 27.5 hours of effort—but that's real world—and the elephant in the living room! (Talk about this with your sponsor and stakeholders at your peril.)

Efficiency Ratios

The project manager develops the costs based on the Gantt Chart (calendar time spent), but develops a realistic schedule using effort hours and converting to duration using a realistic efficiency ratio.

On-the-ground project management is like the making of sausages and laws—you like the results, but you shouldn't bother to look at the process of creating—you might never eat sausage again and may be permanently soured by all the backroom deals cut to pass needed legislation. This is a technique we do not announce to the sponsor and stakeholders—it's that elephant that no one wants to see or acknowledge—but deep down they know its there—they just won't admit it.

This is how we schedule our project. The 27.5-hour figure is known as the productivity level, while 27.5 divided by 40 or .6875 is known as the efficiency ratio. However, the .6875 ratio does not take into account sick/personal time (2 days per person per month). When that is added in, the ratio drops to about .5975.

For a 9-hour day, 8 to 5 or 9 to 6, we subtract 5 (lunch) from 45 to arrive at 40. From 40 we subtract 8.25 (longer day, more coffee, etc.), bringing effort hours to 31.75 (productivity level). The efficiency ratio would be .6944. That would allow the average disciplined worker to complete one 20-hour task per week with 11.25 hours left over to start the next task or do something else. With the 2 days per person or sick/personal time per month factored in, the ratio drops to .6156. (See Table 4.16.)

This is how realistic project schedules and time lines are developed. For accuracy, estimate in effort and convert to duration using a realistic efficiency ratio. Why estimate in effort? Because there are fewer variables in effort. There is no inclusion of "Oh, I've been selected to work on a rush project for the company president, so . . ."; "Oh, I can't work full time on the task, so . . ."; "Oh, I have been called away to troubleshoot . . ."; "Oh, what if I get the flu . . ."; "Oh, no child

Table 4.16   Typical Efficiency Ratio Calculations

North East (Exempt Employee) Paid Time by the Book

40-Hour Workweek[a]

Elements	Hours
Workweek	40.0
Lunch	−5.0
Social/maintenance time	−7.5
Total Productivity level (hours available for work)	27.5

45-Hour Workweek[b]

Elements	Hours
Workweek	45.0
Lunch	−5.0
Social/maintenance time	−8.75
Total Productivity level (hours available for work)	31.25

[a] The average, competent worker can complete one 20-hour effort task per week with 7.5 hours left over to start a new task. This implies an efficiency ratio of .6875 (27.5/40.0 = .6875).

[b] The average, competent worker can complete one 20-hour effort task per week with 13.75 hours left over to start a new task. This implies an efficiency ratio of .6944 (31.25/45.0 = .6944).

© Copyright 2007 Pamela McGhee and Peter McAliney.

care available this week, so I'll have to arrive later and leave earlier." All of these real-life variables disappear when effort estimates are used. By applying a realistic efficiency ratio to convert to duration, the project manager can better predict the schedule outcome. (Yes, we are talking about *estimates* here.)

A Short Cut

For a short cut, divide the length of the critical path in effort hours by the efficiency ratio and you will arrive at the number of hours (duration) the work will take.

Why estimate in effort and convert to duration? Here are some of the reasons:

- The project worker/subject matter expert (SMEs) is not really in control of their time. Management is. SMEs could be pulled away from the project at any time, making their duration estimate invalid.
- Effort contains fewer variables than duration. We can avoid the inconvenient trouble shooting incident, the unexpected sick day, and a host of other unanticipated events.
- Estimating in effort forces attention to the actual project work, and de-emphasizes the schedule of an individual project contributor who may, if necessary, be replaced.

TIP

As a rule of thumb, given today's multitasking workplace, unless you have substantive other data, using an efficiency ratio of .5 is prudently optimistic.

The purpose and uses of the Gantt Chart range from Status Reporting, to costing, to tracking project labor hours, to presenting project progress, to determining whether or not the project is on schedule.

The Gantt Chart allows the project manager, the project team, and any and all interested parties to visualize the project and its progress in calendar or time line terms. It can be used to answer questions like: "Are we on time, ahead of or behind schedule?" "How much money has been spent so far?" "How many hours have been devoted to the project?"

While the WBS and the logic diagram are primarily internal project management tools, the Gantt Chart is the project manager's means for external communications to the sponsor, stakeholders, and everyone else.

However, bear in mind that while the Gantt Chart is one of the project manager's main externally focused tools, it is also a vital internal project management tool.

Every project manager should post the current (usually weekly) Gantt Chart (Table 4.17) in an area accessible to project team members. This will keep the schedule on everyone's mind, as well as allowing the project team to monitor and manage itself. The more they

Table 4.17   Gantt Chart Showing Calendar Duration

Task	Resource	Weeks					
		1	2	3	4	5	6
A	Paula	4.36 da					
B	Jerry		1.45 da				
C	Paula		4.36 da				
D	Jane		2.90 da				
E	Steve		7.27 da				
F	Bob				8.72 da		
G	Jerry				5.81 da		
H	Paula				4.36 da		

Day 23

manage themselves, the more empowered they are and the less (over-time) the project manager has to do.

Based on the network diagram (Figure 4.11 on p. 91) on the Gantt Chart, which represents duration, the time to complete the project represented by the network would actually be 23 days if we used an efficiency ratio of .6875.

We do recommend estimating in effort hours and converting to duration using an efficiency ratio based on your organization's work patterns and dynamics.

Developing the Baseline Plan

Eventually, after enough iterations, you'll get to a schedule and cost (Gantt Chart) that hopefully, you as project manager and your stakeholders can live with. This becomes the baseline schedule, which is a part of the IPP.

Once the IPP is passed around and approved, it becomes the Baseline Project Plan. Once that Baseline Plan is approved by those who will pay the bill, you and your project team are ready for the Execution Phase of the project.

It is now time to revisit our road map (Figure 4.6, p. 77). We have completed Planning and are poised for Execution.

TIPS

- **Work with the sponsor and major stakeholders to develop the Business Case.**
- **Without a Charter, you have no steering wheel.**
- **Changes cost time, money, and resources and can occur at any point during the PMLC, during any phase.**
- **Sign-offs from the client are needed at each phase, during the phase, and at key milestone points.**

Execution

The project manager's primary responsibilities during Execution are:

1. The motivation and supervision of the project team;
2. The monitoring of actual progress against the baseline plan;
3. Determining any variances to that plan by collecting work status in a timely and periodic manner;
4. Determining if any action is needed because of any variance in actual progress versus planned progress in terms of schedule or cost or requirements;
5. Taking action if necessary;
6. Handling all changes that come in from outside the project (from the business, the environment external to the business itself, or from the sponsor, stakeholders, clients, or other interested parties); and
7. Handling changes that are produced by the project work itself.

In addition, it is the job of the project manager to issue periodic status reports to all parties (the sponsor, stakeholders, clients, users) including the project team members and other project managers working on related projects as well as any business areas affected by the project and business areas providing input or resources to the project.

It is also the project manager's job to manage all work and resources within the scope of the project and to report on the status of that work. If extra resources, time, or money are needed to deliver the required product or service, it is the project manager's job to procure same either by dipping into the Management Reserve, or by quantifying what is needed and escalating the issues for resolution at a higher level in the organization.

The project manager's power and authority are limited. The savvy project manager knows when to escalate project issues and escalates earlier rather than later, when there is less time to effect a turnaround.

In Execution, the project manager is a disciplined gatekeeper, making certain that planned scope, time, and costs are adhered to. If they are not, it is the project manager's job to resolve the discrepancies or explain to the project owners why the discrepancies cannot be resolved.

Yes, the project manager lives in the hot seat!

Here is a typical Execution (with Monitoring and Control) activities list (or what the project manager does in the Execution phase of her project):

- Hold a "We're 'Building It'" (Execution) Kick-Off Meeting with the sponsor, stakeholders, and other interested parties. Distribute the Baseline Project Plan (high-level). A PowerPoint format is useful. The meeting should be brief and "Ra Ra!"

- Hold a "We're Starting the Work" meeting with the project team doing the work. Make certain that all project workers attend, those working full time on the project as well as those working part time. Use this meeting as a team-building and motivational meeting. Distribute a detailed Baseline Project Plan. Cite each team member's role on the project. Serve something to munch on like cookies or such and have something to drink (water, coffee, juice). Distribute Status Report templates and inform the team when Status Reports on their work are expected. Also distribute a Change Control Form, stating that anyone can submit a change and all changes must flow through you. (As project manager, start a Change Control Log.) Give out some trinket with the project name imprinted on it to each team member. This is particularly meaningful for large, or high profile projects. The savvy project manager starts right away to develop that Gestalt creature, which is a high-functioning project team. Project success may very well depend more on the team than the project manager.

- Don't be overly imbued with your role as project manager. It's about the *team*.
- On the day that work starts, MBWA (Manage By Walking Around).
- Collect status reports as announced.
- Compile the Status Reports and compare the actual progress to the planned progress. In that report, announce any changes needed to keep the project on schedule, within scope and requirements, and on budget. If changes necessary are not within your authority to make, escalate those changes to the sponsor and stakeholders (consult your manager first).
- Distribute the results to all team members in the form of an annotated Gantt Chart, using each team member's name. Include your name as project manager.
- Hold periodic, brief status reporting meetings with the project team. They can be virtual when the project team is not co-located. Geography should not be allowed to be a barrier.
- Distribute a summary Status Report to stakeholders per agreed upon reporting frequency.
- Hold periodic team building, motivational, and problem-solving meetings (build that Gestalt creature!)
- Hold periodic change control sessions to deal with project changes.
- Keep the Change Control Log up to date and cite important changes in the status reports.
- Continue MBWA.
- Repeat actions until product or service is delivered.

If the project manager "executes" this list, it is highly likely that he or she will stay out of major trouble—unless there are extenuating circumstances.

Close (Post Mortem)

After delivering the product or service to the project owners (sponsor, stakeholders, clients, users), and ascertaining that the product or service is working as specified and the owners are able to use it operationally, the project manager, the project team, and the stakeholders (hopefully) conduct the Close (i.e., Post Mortem, or Lessons Learned).

There are several ways to conduct a Close. The project manager for the Close could have been the project manager for the entire project, or a different project manager for the purposes of nonbias and objectivity. There are many Close techniques.

One method is by a written survey sent out to all participants in the project. Each recipient fills out the survey form and returns it to the person conducting the Close. This technique is the least expensive and also produces the least feedback. In addition, much that went on in the project does not easily translate to print.

Another method is to have a Closing meeting, with stakeholders, sponsor, clients, the project manager, and the project team in attendance. The meeting can be facilitated by the project manager or an independent facilitator (the better option). There is a strict agenda, distributed in advance, and a meeting minutes taker present. The meeting may extend over several days, as meetings like this are most effective when they are relatively short (at or under one hour).

Remember, the goal of a Close is to learn from both positive and negative elements of the project.

There are several options: The Close can be conducted by PMLC phases; a Concept Close, followed by a Close for Planning and Execution (including Monitoring and Control).

Also possible is the conducting of the Close by internal and external deliverables, rating the effectiveness of the Business Case, the Project Charter, the Integrated Project Plan, Status Reports, and the timeliness and quality of the product or service produced by the project.

Whichever method used, here are some questions to pose at a Close:

- Was the quality of the product or service produced acceptable?
- Was it delivered on time?
- Were budget expectations met?
- Was the communication between the project manager and the project team adequate?
- Did each team member understand the goals of the project?
- Were there revisions to the Project Charter later on in Planning? Why?
- How well did the project team perform?
- How well did the project manager perform?
- Was there adequate sponsor/stakeholder participation?
- Were the status reports informative and presented at the right level?

By now, you can see that Closes can be sensitive, politically and otherwise. However, if they are not conducted in a serious manner, those same old mistakes will be made over and over. Those who do not study history are condemned to repeat it.

For an easy to use Close template, please visit us at our website http://www.painlessprojectmanagement.info for a free download.

REAL LIFE EXPERIENCES FROM THE TRENCHES

VIGNETTE 4—Putting the Project Life Cycle to Work in Higher Education

As a large, public college in a major urban area, our mission is to serve the needs of our community. Since our community represents a very diverse underlying population, these needs can be varied and wide. As the associate dean of the continuing and professional studies division, my job is to work with different segments of the community to put together specific programs that help the college deliver on its mission. Initiating, managing, and seeing these initiatives through to completion are greatly assisted using a project management framework. Take the program we just launched to set up a college within a private high school whereby students took college level courses in their high school while earning credits from our institution.

As some background, the college was interested in attracting higher quality students from diverse backgrounds within the community. An increased admissions pool would attract better faculty and endowments, which in turn would provide for a better education for all students attending the college. This fit well within the college's mission. We were approached by a private high school that represented a specific ethnic and religious population within the community. From their perspective, they were interested in having their students receive college credits while still in high school. Ultimately, they wanted their students to attend our college so they could finish their college education in four years or less (a challenge for public colleges due to course scheduling and fluctuating demand). For the college, this relationship meant we would have increased access to a student population that fit within our mission.

In our initial meetings, I met with members of the high school's lay leadership and administration. Both sides brought different biases to the conversations, but as we discussed the college's vision and the high school's vision, we soon established a joint vision for the project's concept that was "our" vision. We were careful to make sure the mission statement for the project was aligned with both the college and high school's mission statements. We established specific goals, project scope, objectives, success factors, and other measurements that created a project that we both owned. The agreement in concept for this project was completed in the spring and we were looking for a September start. To assure this would happen, we knew we would need to depend on the application of good project management protocols.

Having agreed on the project concept, we then proceeded to put a plan together. This plan had to include coordinating schedules across the high school and the college, hiring faculty, establishing standards for grading, determining acceptance criteria for students, determining costs for the program, identifying possible outside funding sources to support the venture, and a host of other very real world, logistical details. An important part of this planning stage included making sure we secured buy-in from major stakeholder groups. If you have ever worked in a public college, you can appreciate that this is not always that straight forward. Getting the provost, registrar, bursar, college attorney, and department chairs on the same page, aligned, and motivated to all move in the same direction is perhaps one of the biggest challenges in higher education—especially when it is a public institution. Engaging all the stakeholders in the planning stage was very important to make sure they were committed to the timetable required for successful implementation.

Having developed and received approval for the initial project plan, we were now ready to get down to the organizing and scheduling involved. Here, we had to tap into the people who were actually going to make this happen—the folks on the "front lines." This meant working with the schedulers to coordinate classes, identify and hire instructors who had their own constraints to deal with, getting the office of finance to set up an entire new set of accounts to track the costs and revenues for the project, select and modify courses that could be delivered in a format to high school students, and process immunization records to meet state requirements. This involved front-line personnel from both the high school and the college. We identified a number of work streams that we would have to work simultaneously and identified the critical path activities that were crucial for accomplishing to meet our September implementation.

As the project got underway, we were continually checking the work against the schedules established. Slippage occurred (when have you been on a project where slippage has *not* occurred!). Because the legal work stream and implementation work stream were running currently, with a month to go before implementation, we were informed of additional criteria that needed to be met in relationship to class size. This required issuing the equivalent of a change order to the scheduler at our high school partner to make sure we would be in compliance with the demands made by the legal department. Weekly conference calls—and as we got closer to implementation, daily conference calls—between the major players assured that the project was heading for the defined outcomes as laid out in the project plan.

September rolled around and the project was launched. Ten courses were launched at the college within the high school. We are still working through some of the implementation issues but without the tools of project planning, we never could have expected to see such a successful launch. In doing the Project Close—an often missed opportunity, as I see it—we were able to take the learning from our project and structure the outline of a model that we are now taking to other specific high schools in the community that our college serves. Using the accumulated knowledge from this project, we will be able to implement more of these "college within a high school" programs and fulfill the educational mission of our college to the community.

LILLIAN O'REILLY
Associate Dean,
Large Urban Public College

THE PAINLESS TRIED-AND-TRUE METHOD FOR LARGER, MORE COMPLEX PROJECTS AND EXPERIENCED PROJECT MANAGERS

If you have been managing projects for a while (and have most of the basics mastered) and are ready to graduate to managing larger, more complex projects, or if you have been thrown into a complex project, the management of which requires more sophisticated tools and techniques, Part II is for you. (However, it wouldn't hurt to take a quick pass at Part I first.)

CHAPTER 5

Developing the Project Charter for Larger, More Complex Projects

The Project Charter is the first step in the development of the Project Plan. The more complex and complicated the project is, the greater the need for a detailed and unambiguous Charter. In addition, the more "real estate" (business areas and a multiplicity of stakeholders) the project covers, the more hands must be involved in its development and the more reviews and revisions it will go through. The project manager may need to assume the role of lion tamer, or at the very least, referee. While the material in the Charter comes from or is generated by the sponsor and stakeholders, the project manager is the willing interpreter and scribe, and at times, has valuable contributions to make.

Figure 5.1 is the "big picture" of the Planning process from Part I of this book. Developing the Charter is the "kick-off" to the rest of the Planning process.

A project needs boundaries. It will neither encompass nor do everything. What's in? What's out? Who's in? Who's out? How much? How long? What is success? How do you measure success? Who makes decisions? What is quality? All those associated with the project—the stakeholders—must have a common understanding about

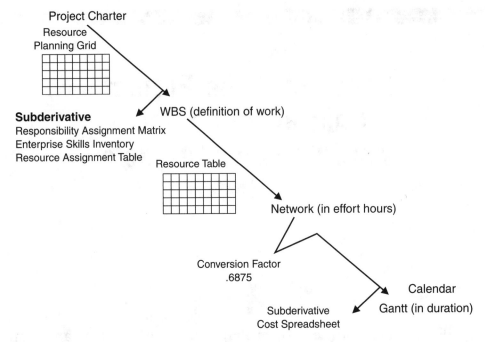

Figure 5.1   The Evolution of a Project Plan. © Copyright 2007 Pamela McGhee and Peter McAliney.

the project. They need to share a common set of assumptions around many things. They need to have a common reference that will enable them to answer questions about a project's inputs, work processes, resources, and outputs. They need a framework within which to manage their expectations.

The answers to these questions are in a jointly developed document called the Project Charter, a document that is written by and for the stakeholders of the project.

Project Stakeholders

The individuals inside or outside an organization who impact or who are impacted by a project are called *stakeholders*. A key role of the project manager is to manage these stakeholders. Typical project stakeholders include:

- *Client:* Receives product of the project. Approves deliverables, articulates requirements. May be on Change Review Board (see Chapter 7).

- *Project team:* Those directly responsible for delivering the product of the project. May be a cross-functional team and can include outside consultants or members of supplier organizations.

- *Project sponsor:* An individual—or a group—who provides resources and direction for the project manager as they relate to the completion of the project. Serves as advisor to the project manager. Approves the Charter, thus establishing a contract defining the work of the project. Will sit on—and often chair—the Change Review Board (see Chapter 7).

- *Discipline specific (functional) or geographic managers:* Supply resources and/or skills to project as directed by the project sponsor. May provide subject matter expertise. May be on Change Review Board (see Chapter 7).

- *Vendors/suppliers:* Provide inputs to the project. Can be goods (e.g., computer hardware/software/telecom equipment, raw materials for manufacturing processes, computer support systems) or services (e.g., consulting support, training).

- *The project manager:* As alluded to earlier, the "cat herder." Expert in all matters of consequence as they relate to the project.

Many times, stakeholder needs will conflict. As the project manager begins to develop the project's Charter, he or she should take the time to get to know the needs, wants, desires, and anxieties of the project's stakeholders. An important tool to help the project manager develop an understanding of the stakeholders is the stakeholder analysis chart (Table 5.1), which he or she should begin to

Table 5.1   Stakeholder Analysis Chart

Stakeholder Group	Individual	Potential Issues	Potential Conflicts with Other Stakeholders
Project team	Person A		
	Person B		
	…		
	Person X		
Customer	Key contact A		
	Key contact B		
	…		
	Key contact X		
Sponsor	Sponsor A		
	Sponsor B		
	…		
	Sponsor X		
Company managers	Functional		
	Geographical		
	…		
	Manager X		
Vendors/suppliers	Vendor A		
	Vendor B		
	…		
	Vendor X		

compile. This is the beginning of the project manager's understanding about what he or she must do to keep stakeholders engaged and contributing to the project. This chart will be developed further in Chapter 6.

Role of the Project Charter

The Project Charter is the document that brings a project to life. It is developed by the project sponsor, major stakeholders, and those who will use the final product or service. The project manager functions as a catalyst, guide, contributor, and scribe. The project manager reaches out to a number of individuals (stakeholders and those with relevant project or product/service-related information) in the organization to help him or her compile the Project Charter. As noted, the project sponsor approves the Charter.

TIP

The initial group of people the project manager reaches out to will be few in number but that number will grow as the Charter develops. The development of the Charter is as much about defining the project as it is about empowering stakeholders and gaining buy-in.

Elements of the Project Charter

Table 5.2 is a sample Project Charter outline as an alternative format to the Charter template in Table 4.2 on page 59. The Charter can be short (small, simple project) or quite lengthy (large, complex, mission-critical project). In every case, it provides an unambiguous definition of

Table 5.2 Sample Project Charter Outline for Larger, More Complex Projects

Project Name

Date Prepared

Prepared By

Revision Log

Approvals

Table of Contents

Executive Summary

Corporate Mission

Project Mission

Business Case
  –Background
  –Project rationale
  –Project goal
  –Objectives
  –Critical success factors
  –Critical success measures

Assumptions

Project Scope
  –Solution development
  –Implementation and integration
  –Production migration
  –Decommission
  –Exclusions

Risks

Constraints

Stakeholders

Project Team Structure

Commitment to Quality

Communications and Reporting

Appendices
  –Preliminary budget analysis
  –Project labor requirements analysis

the project, agreed to by all involved. The following elements are a part of an expanded Project Charter:

- *Project name:* This is the unique identifier that people in the organization will use when referring to a project. For smaller projects, this is not such an important element, but for larger projects, this can serve the purpose of developing an esprit de corps around a major initiative. For example, a project I worked on for a major electric utility that faced the loss of the largest client in its rate base—the U.S. Navy—was appropriately named "Save the Navy."

- *Date prepared:* An important first step in a project is getting the first internal deliverable completed in a timely fashion. Assigning the Charter completion date establishes a fixed reference point for a project for all who are involved with the project.

- *Prepared by:* In the Project Charter, the key individuals who contributed to the development of the Charter are listed, as well as the name of the project manager. Including others' names in the Project Charter serves the purpose of exhibiting to the organization the breadth of talent that was employed in the development of the Charter. Especially when a project is boundary spanning (i.e., includes multiple departments within an organization), representation from the different departments involved illustrates the collaborative nature of the proposed project. This can be instrumental in obtaining higher-level organizational approval.

- *Revision log:* As the project progresses, changes in scope may be necessitated due to changes in internal project circumstances, business needs, or other project-altering events. It is important to track changes in the project's scope, schedule, and costs so that the project manager can manage stakeholders' expectations. This also can provide an audit trail that will be helpful for any new players who join the project team.

- *Approvals:* In its role as a contract, the appropriate parties need to understand, agree to, and sign off their expectations of the project.

Appropriate approvals might include clients, stakeholders, the project sponsor, major vendors, and, of course, the project manager.

- *Table of contents:* Simple, but necessary, the table of contents allows ready reference to any stakeholder who needs to revisit or review elements of the Project Charter.

- *Executive summary:* Gives a high level view of the project. While physically appearing as the first substantive description of the project, it is actually the last part of the Project Charter that is completed. The executive summary needs to summarize the important benefits, processes, and resources associated with a project. In reality, it is often the only part of the Charter read by many. It should be accurate, pithy, and short.

- *Corporate mission:* Because a project should be undertaken only in support of enhancing the company's mission (strategic alignment), the project team needs to illustrate their understanding of the company's mission. We have seen intended projects never get birthed after the project team truly understands the mission of the organization.

- *Project mission:* A short articulation of the project needs to be provided. This section should also show how the specified project will contribute to the organization's mission articulated in the prior section.

- *Business Case:* The Business Case states the reason why the project is important for the company. It shows that the return for the project will meet or exceed the return required by the organization. There are six elements to the Business Case:

  1. *Background:* Provides the context for the project. Who are the major players? What are the major issues facing the organization? The industry? What is the industry life cycle stage (e.g., embryonic, growth, shakeout, mature, declining)?

  2. *Project rationale:* What are the organizational needs that are not being met? What would be the impact of not undertaking

the defined project? What should the reader know about the organization, the industry, the economy, the technology, the resources, and other relevant things that call for a project such as the one in the Project Charter to be initiated?

3. *Project goal:* What does the organization hope to achieve in undertaking the project? Will it reduce costs? Will it increase revenues? Will it reduce cycle time?

4. *Objectives:* What are the specific, measurable areas that will communicate that the project's goals are being met? These fall into two categories:

5. *Critical success factors:* Those project objectives that *must* be accomplished in order for the project to have fulfilled its goals.

6. *Critical success measures:* Ways to measure if the critical success factors are being met. Values for these need to be articulated in advance to determine if the project Critical Success Factors will be accomplished.

- *Assumptions:* Those set of givens that need to be articulated to all stakeholders. Developing the list of assumptions can be a very revealing exercise because it provides wonderful insights that reveal stakeholder biases. Assumptions should be discussed with individual stakeholder groups first. If some assumptions are very disparate, it is sometimes necessary to call a meeting of different stakeholder groups to hammer out the assumptions.

TIP

As tempting as it is to let differences of assumptions remain unresolved at this early stage for fear of alienating stakeholder groups, it is imperative to get these differences resolved early. It will always be more costly to do so at a later stage in time.

- *Project scope:* Simply stated, what's in and what's out. If you have ever heard the expression "scope creep," this refers to the insidious tendency for projects to try to do more and more and more. Imagine setting out to build a modest, two-story house and ending up with Windsor Castle! There are five elements of the project scope:

  1. *Solution development:* An outline of the elements that make up the solution.

  2. *Implementation and integration:* If the project is an improvement of a process, how the results/deliverables of the project will be put into place within the organization. This usually contains a pilot stage (i.e., implementation on a small scale whereby kinks can be worked out of the system) before full-scale implementation.

  3. *Production migration:* If the project is an improvement of a process, how the project's deliverables will move from pilot stage to the new way a company conducts business.

  4. *Decommission:* If the project is an improvement of a process, how the older process will be removed from the organization.

  5. *Exclusions:* What will *not* be done. This is the element of scope for which the term "scope creep" was created.

In addition, the Project Charter contains a discussion of the following:

- *Risks:* Like many elements of the Charter, the project manager's view of risk becomes clearer as time passes. A model for thinking about project risk is illustrated in Table 5.3.

- *Constraints:* You want to describe internal structural or any other constraints that you must work within to accomplish the project. It is important to articulate constraints to help manage stakeholder expectations.

Table 5.3   Potential Sources of Project Risk

Project Related Risks	Partner Related Risks
–Scheduling	–Financial difficulty
–Cost	–Change in ownership
–Personnel—individual	–Nonperformance
–Personnel—team	–Cost increase
–Quality	–Key contact personnel turnover
–Stakeholders (internal)	
–Scope change	
–Management	
Business Related Risks	**External Risks**
–Contract difficulties	–Industry
–Market shift	–Environmental
–Competitor activity	–Political
–Technology shifts	–Cultural
–Customer demand	–Social

© Copyright 2007 Pamela McGhee and Peter McAliney.

- *Stakeholders:* See the previous discussion of stakeholders.

- *Project team structure:* A team can have many structures: hierarchical, matrix, project matrix, tiger team, skunk works (see Chapter 8). There is no one correct design but pick the one that makes the most sense and make sure everyone understands what it is.

- *Commitment to quality:* The Charter should document what the project's commitment to quality is. Whereas most projects will want to meet or exceed the company's or industry standards, there may be instances where this is not the case. For example, an organization may be willing to relax its usual quality standards in order to implement a short-term, fast turnaround fix.

- *Communications and reporting:* The philosophy and an outline of a communications and reporting plan need to be articulated in the Project Charter. As the project plan unfolds, the level of detail in the communications plan will become much greater (see Chapters 6 and 7).

- *Appendices:* Depending on the project, the Charter can have any number of general or specific appendices. Two appendices that should minimally appear in a project plan are:

  1. *Preliminary budget analysis:* Some estimation of the project's cost. At this point, it is sometimes adequate to have a cost range for the project cost.

  2. *Project labor requirements analysis:* Some estimate of the number and type of resources, whether these are available internally or must be acquired from outside the organization, and for how long they will be required to staff the project.

Tools for Developing Lists

When it comes to generating lists for Charter items such as stakeholder issues and project risks, a project manager should develop a list that is as robust as possible—he or she does not want to take this step lightly. There are a number of useful tools the project manager can employ to develop comprehensive lists for the creation of the Charter including:

- *Historical information:* Look through Project Close reports from other projects that the organization undertook that are applicable to the current project. Speak with colleagues in other departments who have run projects.

- *Vendor/Suppliers:* Speak with vendors and suppliers to see what they have seen in working with other clients.

- *Brainstorming:* Provide a comfortable and detached environment for a cross-functional group of individuals to get together to think creatively. Food and refreshments ALWAYS help.

- *Delphi technique:* Send out questionnaires to those you believe would have some insight about the project. Receive questionnaires back, organize and sort them, and then resend them to the participants for additional thoughts.

- *Forced ranking (or nominal group technique):* Assemble a group of individuals and ask them to list the most important thing they can think about (i.e., biggest issue for a stakeholder group, largest risk factor). Have them write it on a sticky note. Collect the notes and place them in full view. Go around the room again, asking for items that the group has not yet generated. Continue the process until all ideas are exhausted.

Project Charter Sign-Off

Before embarking on the project, you will want the project stakeholders to sign off on the project. The Charter, as we had mentioned before, serves as a contract. In having all of the stakeholders sign off on the Project Charter, you are holding them accountable for having read and understood the purpose, process, and deliverables that will result at the end of the project. Their signatures represent their commitment to the completion of the project and their cooperation to contribute as spelled out in the Charter.

TIP

After all signatures are obtained on the Project Charter, the project manager should photocopy the original and provide copies to all stakeholders.

Conclusion

The Charter is complete. The stakeholders have contributed to its development and have signed off. It's now time for the project kick-off meeting.

REAL LIFE EXPERIENCES FROM THE TRENCHES

VIGNETTE 5—The "Real" Process of Developing the Charter: Chartering

We've all heard the expression "talk is cheap." In the world of project management, it is the charter that serves as the mechanism for converting talk into action. It is at this point, that a formerly unrelated group of individuals inside and outside the organization are pulled together to begin sharing the common name of stakeholder for a specific project.

I was working with a Visual Effects House on a major redesign initiative. The client produced visual effects for large motion picture studios. The nature of the work was such that it employed anywhere from 5 to 15 artistic crafts to create the different effects that the studios demanded. And, yes, artistic types are, as you might surmise from common knowledge, well . . . artistic (translated, they have a passion for their art and not necessarily the business component for delivering their art). Since the movie-going public was demanding more and more visual effects in movies, it had started to become a major line item cost for the studios. This attracted their attention.

Studio executives started to demand more cost-effective visual effects from the Visual Effects House. Management of the Visual Effects House knew that if they did not redesign the way visual effects were created, there stood the potential that they would start losing projects to smaller, more agile companies who did not have the overhead responsibilities that they did as one of the largest visual effects companies. They met with me to discuss what could be done. As a result of numerous conversations, management decided they needed to initiate a major redesign project to help deliver their visual effects better, faster, and cheaper than they had in the past. They realized that in order to do so, they would have to engage the 15 or so artist groups who collaboratively produced the effects to see the importance of the initiative and, more important, help develop new work processes. I suggested that the first stage of the project should be to create a lead team containing a representative group of managers, producers, artists, and other creatives to jointly develop a Project Charter for the initiative.

The charter had to address the needs of all major constituencies. Artists and other creatives wanted the freedom to develop new and "cooler" techniques employing the latest bleeding edge (and expensive) technology. Producers were accountable to management to bring in the work on time and on budget—a budget that their client movie studios were telling them now had to be less than what it was in the past. The charter that was to be developed had to address seemingly contradictory demands. And in the many projects that I have worked on in my career (spanning many different industries), managing contradictory demands is *always* part of developing the charter.

While there is much talk of the charter as a document, I think the power of the charter is in the verb form—chartering. The process of bringing together a group of people—sometimes with divergent and even adversarial viewpoints—to focus their attention on solving a business imperative is an exciting and challenging activity. It often involves educating the different parties about what their needs, constraints, and worries are. Many times, groups find that they share similar constraints and worries and they are more like than un-like. It's about forming relationships, building trust, finding out about complementary skills, and, oh yes, producing a document called the charter.

STEPHEN H. BAUM
The Point Group Network

CHAPTER 6

Much, Much, More on WBSs, Networks, and Gantt Charts

The Charter is now complete. Everyone agrees what needs to be done. As they say, the "devil is in the details" and now it's time to get to the details.

If you have never managed a project before—or even if you have, but not to the scale of your present project—you may be a little daunted as to where to begin. After the initial euphoria of the Charter signing wears off, you may experience what we professionals call a "Yikes" moment, as in, "Yikes! What do I do now?" A good project manager at this point will take a deep breath, collect his or her thoughts, go to his or her tool kit, and begin to start digging into the details of planning the project.

At this point, the project manager has to develop more detail around:

- What the work is.
- How long it will take.
- How much it will cost.
- Who will do the work.
- What could go wrong (i.e., risks revisited).

In order to do this, you must develop a Work Breakdown Structure (WBS).

This needs to be articulated at an increasing level of detail as the work of the project begins. Not to be caught in the paradigm of "analysis paralysis," a good project manager undertakes the description of the details using an iterative approach, providing more detail and obtaining more buy-in each time the work of the project is more fully defined. *The iterative approach brings clarity to the project plan and enhances communication among stakeholders.* We call this "helicoptering in."

A project needs boundaries. It will neither encompass nor do everything. What's in? What's out? Who's in? Who's out? How much? How long? What is success? How do you measure success? Who makes decisions? What is quality? All those associated with the project—the stakeholders—must have a common understanding about the project. They need to share a common set of assumptions around many things. They need to have a common reference that will enable them to answer questions about a project's inputs, work processes, resources, and outputs. They need a framework within which to manage their expectations. Figure 6.1 illustrates the Helicopter Approach to project planning that will guide you into a secure project start every time.

First Iteration—5,000 Feet

The first step in defining the detail should be to draw a general outline of what the project looks like. The project manager will want to start developing a picture about what the work is, how long it will take, how much it will cost, who will do the work, what could go wrong, and what to do about it. The first picture should describe the steps in the project (i.e., what the work is) in very broad brushstrokes. The additional attributes can then be layered onto this initial picture.

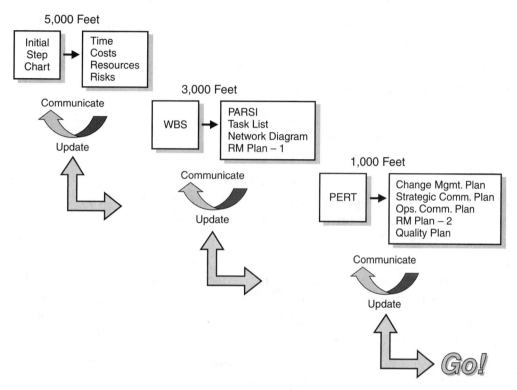

Figure 6.1   The Helicopter Approach to Project Planning. © Copyright 2007 Pamela McGhee and Peter McAliney.

Using the logic of "first do this, then do that, then after that do that . . . ," develop a high level view (i.e., the 5,000-foot view) of the project. Block the project into five to seven very high-level steps. Use a declarative phrase to fill in each of the blocks such that you can describe the project in simplified terms (see Figure 6.2).

The fact that there are potentially hundreds of details under each of these simplified steps is of no concern for the project manager at this time. All that will come—later.

Once the high-level picture is developed, the project manager can then enhance the initial view of the project with the other defining attributes of how long it will take, how much it will cost, who will do the work, what could go wrong, and what to do about it. With this

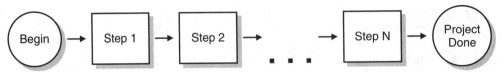

Figure 6.2 The Initial Step Chart. © Copyright 2007 Pamela McGhee and Peter McAliney.

view of the project, it is best not to think in terms of exactness—it is much too early for that—but rather direction and some measure of quantification. Best at this point to think about the project attributes in terms of ranges. Because you know from the Project Charter when the targeted completion date is, how much has been budgeted, and generally what resources are available, you can use these as the basis for developing your 5,000-foot view. You can now develop a high level view of the project as illustrated in Figure 6.3. You will return to this framework two more times as you further refine the project plan.

Using the first high level of the picture will also help you think about what potential problems can occur. Here, you will want to revisit the project, partner, business, and global risks you identified when you were developing the Charter. You can now start to develop a better understanding of them and the impact they can potentially have on the project. With this added level of detail around project steps, you may discount some of the risks you identified earlier in the development of the Charter. Additionally, you may also identify additional risks that were not clear during the Charter development stage.

With this increased knowledge of risk, you can now begin to think about how likely it is that a potential risk will occur. During this first iteration, you should begin to classify—not yet quantify—the likelihood of risk occurring in each of the steps that you have identified in your first block diagram. Using the original risk identification chart that was developed during the Charter, you want to now add a column to capture your estimates of risk by assigning them a value of high, medium, or low to the identified risk. Table 6.1 represents the enhanced risk profile for Step 1 of your project. You will need to plan for risks that might occur and will do this when you develop your risk mitigation contingency plan.

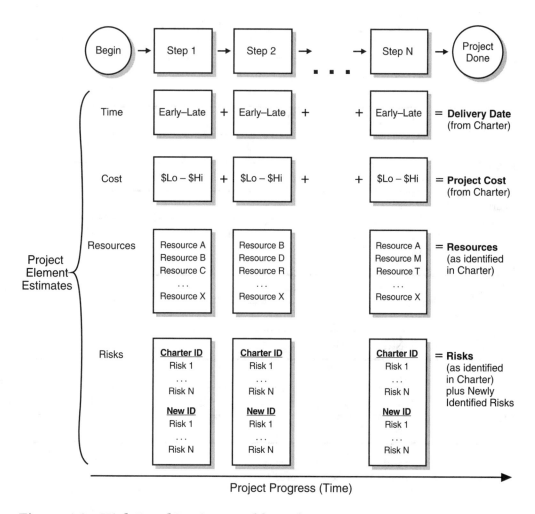

Figure 6.3   High Level Project Dashboard. © Copyright 2007 Pamela McGhee and Peter McAliney.

One of the reasons for approaching the work in this fashion (i.e., top down) is to make sure that resources are not needlessly expended on developing out the work before the work is agreed on by major project stakeholders. For this reason, before adding any more detail to the project plan, you will want to review it with key project stakeholders. You can be sure that valuable refinements will be added when this first cut picture of the project plan is socialized

Table 6.1   Step 1 Risk Identification Chart

Risk Category	Project Risk		Probability
Project	1...		M
			H
	N...		L
Partner	1...		L
			H
	N...		H
Business	1...		M
			M
	N...		M
External	1...		L
			L
	N...		H

© Copyright 2007 Pamela McGhee and Peter McAliney.

among the stakeholders. Incorporate the changes that reflect the spirit of the Charter. For those refinements not incorporated, you will want to get back to the individuals who suggested them. Let them know why a particular enhancement was not included. This must be handled diplomatically. You do not want any of your major stakeholders "checking out" of the process—especially this early in the project.

You are now ready to take the project plan to the next level of detail.

TIP

This first block diagram, along with the associated information, also serves as an important communication tool. Setting up blocks associated with milestones begins to focus the project team on the important components, interim deliverables, and specific risks of the project.

Second Iteration—3,000 Feet

Once the high-level enhanced picture of the project is developed, you can now begin to start drilling into each of the individual pieces that are defined in the project work steps. Remembering that work on any project is done for the sole purpose of creating deliverables, we now have to start thinking about what the deliverables of the project need to be. There are two kinds of deliverables:

1. *Interim deliverables:* Deliverables generated during the course of a project that are necessary inputs to end product deliverables.
2. *End-product deliverables:* Deliverables generated during the course of a project that are part of the solution delivered to the client.

Sometimes, projects tend to overlook the importance of interim deliverables because they are not seen by the client. Beware, however, of neglecting the importance of these interim deliverables. More than one project has gotten into trouble because the project manager took his or her eye off the creation of interim deliverables.

Work Breakdown Structure

A common tool used by project managers to identify the project deliverables is the WBS tool. The WBS graphically illustrates the project's deliverables in an organized and hierarchical fashion. By going through this exercise, and breaking the deliverables into smaller units (or subprojects, if you will), the project starts to become more manageable. Common project management protocol is to use nouns or past-tense events in the WBS (action verbs are reserved for defining tasks, the work component that occurs after the WBS is laid out). In the following example, we illustrate the development of the WBS.

Let's say one of the steps you described for your project was the securing of airtime from a radio station to advertise the new product you are launching. We would call this step "Radio Airtime Project." To secure the airtime, you would have had to identify and produce three deliverables: price quotes, the contract, schedule of times to run advertisements. Each of these deliverables, in turn, might have deliverables under them that need to be identified and produced. So, if we were to look at the deliverable "schedule of times to run advertisements," you would further need to produce deliverables around station demographics, the day-by-day programming schedule, and other advertisers on the station. We could then look at each of these deliverables and determine if there are any other deliverables that support them until we are at a level of deliverable that corresponds to one (work) task.

The WBS corresponding to the "Radio Airtime Project" step in our example is illustrated in Figure 6.4.

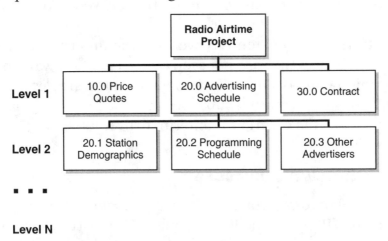

Figure 6.4   Radio Airtime Project. © Copyright 2007 Pamela McGhee and Peter McAliney.

A couple of additional notes about the WBS:

- You will want to limit the number of components under a WBS to between 5 and 7, otherwise the definition of the work will become too difficult to parcel out.

- A coding structure (numbering schema) is important to keeping the work organized in a WBS. It allows you to track both the progress and the cost of the work. Thus, level 1 might start with 10 and increase in increments of 10 with one level of decimalization. Level 2, builds off level 1 and will add a second level of decimalization. Level 3 builds off level 2 and will add a third level of decimalization and so on. Figure 6.5 shows how the coding structure for this project would be carried out through the fifth level of decimalization.

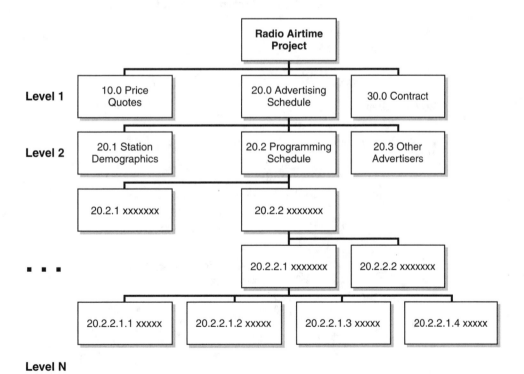

Figure 6.5 WBS Coding Structure. © Copyright 2007 Pamela McGhee and Peter McAliney.

- You may hear some project managers speaking about something called a *work packet*. In one dialect of project management parlance, the lowest level of a WBS is called a work packet. (In another dialect, it is called a task.) What is important to know about a work packet is that it is a unit of work that can be parceled out to a subcontractor or an outside entity. For large projects, this work packet itself can be a pretty significant piece of work.

- Do note that this numbering schema is universal, and follows the basic rules of outlining. If you have a 20.2.1, you must also have a 20.2.2. If there is no legitimate 20.2.2, then 20.2.1 roles up to 20.2.

- While a standard WBS is presented in a graphic format, it can also be displayed in a tree structure (outline form). Some may find this easier to follow (see Table 6.2).

Table 6.2   Radio Airtime Project

10.0 Price Quotes
    10.1 xxxxxxxx
    . . .
    10.N xxxxxxxx

20.0 Advertising Schedule
    20.1 Station demographics
    20.2 Programming schedule
        20.2.1 xxxxxxxx
        20.2.2 xxxxxxxx
            20.2.2.1 xxxxxxxx
                20.2.2.1.1 xxxxxxxx
                20.2.2.1.2 xxxxxxxx
                20.2.2.1.3 xxxxxxxx
                20.2.2.1.4 xxxxxxxx
            20.2.2.2 xxxxxxxx
    20.3 Other advertisers

30.0 Contract
    30.1 xxxxxxxx
    . . .
    30.N xxxxxxxx

When you are developing the WBS, you might find items (work components) that did not originally account for every deliverable that might emerge from the project. *Do not worry—this is actually a good thing.* The iterative approach that you are going through is meant to help you bring clarity to your project. After some discussion, you may decide that the (interim) deliverable belongs in the project. If this is the case, you need to revisit the scope statement and account for this new work component. Alternately, you may decide that the deliverable does not belong in the project. In this case, you will still want to document the fact that this was uncovered but consciously left out of the project. At all times, you want to maintain a complete audit trail for your project work.

Responsibility-Accountability Map

Once you have the deliverables defined, you need to understand what kind of relationship the project players have with them. A project management tool that can present this to you in a concise format is the Responsibility-Accountability Map (some of you who are familiar with project management may also have heard this called the Responsibility Matrix, Responsibility-Accountability Matrix, or the Responsibility-Assignment Matrix). Simply put, the Responsibility-Accountability Map lists the deliverables and defines what responsibility project stakeholders have for the deliverable. This responsibility can take one of five levels of ownership with the deliverable. From weakest to strongest relationship, they are:

1. Communications/FYI only
2. Participates
3. Assists
4. Responsible
5. Sign-off

A tool such as the Responsibility-Accountability Map not only helps focus stakeholders' attention on their contributions to the project, but is also a powerful communications tool that is invaluable in helping to manage individual stakeholders' expectations. Table 6.3 illustrates a sample Responsibility-Accountability Map for the Radio Airtime Project.

A couple of notes about the Responsibility-Accountability Map:

- For each deliverable, there should be only one person who is ultimately responsible. There can, however, be more than one sign-off required, especially for a large resource commitment (see contract sign-off).

- Project members have different contributions to the overall project. Thus, on some parts of the project they will only have a "C"

Table 6.3   Sample Responsibility-Accountability Map

Deliverable/Project Member	Price Quote	Advertising Schedule	Station Demos	Program Schedule	Other Advertisers	Contract
Recording engineer	—	—	—	—	C	—
Marketing assistant	R	R	P	R	R	I
Product manager	A	S	R	S	S	A
Division manager	I	I	S	I	I	R
Research and development	—	—	—	—	I	—
Publicity	—	—	—	I	I	—
Legal	—	—	—	—	—	S
Controller	—	—	—	—	—	S

Note: P = Participates; A = Assists; R = Responsible; S = Sign-off; I = Communications/FYI only.
© Copyright 2007 Pamela McGhee and Peter McAliney.

relationship but on other parts of the project they could have many R and S responsibilities.

Work Behind the Deliverables—Task Lists

It is now time to start talking about the actual work. There is a three-step process to developing the task list, as shown in Figure 6.6.

Step 1 and Step 2

The work consists of a number of tasks that can be independent or somehow related. Initially, we will not be concerned with dependencies.

When constructing the task list, you can choose to approach the job in one of two ways (this is why Figure 6.6 illustrates that Step 1 and Step 2 can be ordered in one of two ways):

1. *By step:* Identifying work tasks as they relate to the different steps in the project first. This approach would take the WBS units and organize them according to work step.

2. *By discipline:* Identifying work as it relates to disciplines. This approach would take the WBS units and organize them according to different disciplines that contribute on the project.

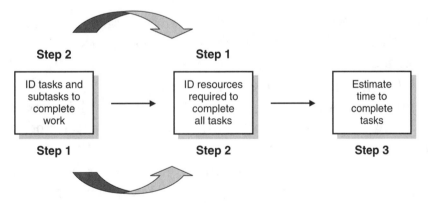

Figure 6.6 Developing Task Lists. © Copyright 2007 Pamela McGhee and Peter McAliney.

One way is not any better than the other. They each have their advantages and you will end up at the same spot at the end of the project. If you choose to lead by task, you will eventually have to assign disciplines to completing the work. If you choose to lead by discipline, you will eventually have to overlay the work into the steps. It is important at this point in time to simply list all of the tasks that you think will be necessary. Under the paradigm of an iterative approach, recognize that some may be pruned later while others will be added.

TIP

Engage the project team in creating the task lists. This will provide a sense of ownership and will help manage expectations.

Step 3

We can now revisit the time estimates we initially developed. There is no scientific way to estimate how long it will take to complete tasks. There are a few guidelines you can follow, however:

- *Use history:* Has the organization ever done anything like this before (here is where good organizational project management recordkeeping can assist you—see Chapter 7).
- *Use benchmarks:* Reach out to your network (e.g., former colleagues, professional organizations, prior consulting companies you may have used). Do a quick scan of industry and project management literature.
- *Bottom up—top down:* Come up with estimates by figuring out how long individual tasks will take and add them up. Look back to the Charter and the view from 5,000 feet to see how much time you have available. This way you will develop an integrated view.

Ordering the Tasks—The Network Diagram

At this point, you have identified tasks (and subtasks), assigned resources and time estimates. Now it's time to start seeing how all these tasks fit together. Tasks can either be independent (have no relationship with each other) or dependent. If tasks are dependent, they usually are related in one of the following three ways:

1. *Finish to start:* The independent task must *finish* before the dependent task *starts.* A simple example would be if you were changing a tire, you must first unfasten all of the nuts (the independent task) before you can take the rim off the car (the dependent task).

2. *Finish to finish:* The independent task must *finish* before the dependent task *finishes.* A simple example of this is if you are building a house, you need to have the frame up before you put the roof on. Assuming the roof will rest on the frame, you cannot put the roof on until the framing is complete. You can, however, build a prefabricated roof to set on the frame so that once the frame is completed, the prefabricated roof can be set on top of the finished frame.

3. *Start to start:* The independent task must *start* before the dependent task *starts.* A simple example of this would be if you were writing documentation for a product or service (e.g., software, consumer, commercial), you can review the documentation materials as they are being written. You do not have to wait until the end to start reviewing materials.

Your job at this point in time is to review the task lists you have created and start organizing them according to the relationship they have with each other. You can think of organizing the project's tasks into subprojects, wherein some of the subprojects are related to other subprojects and some subprojects are completely independent. In project management, we call this creating the network diagram.

Simply put, a network diagram is a picture that illustrates the order in which tasks will be done (if you are familiar with a flow chart, then you can think about a network diagram as a flow chart that maps task activity). Just like a project has a beginning and an end point, so too, do the tasks associated with the subprojects within a project. You will want to organize the tasks in a logical sequence such that the beginning point is represented on the left of the chart and the result is represented on the right of the chart. While there are a couple of different ways that network diagrams can be presented visually, Figure 6.7 illustrates a network diagram showing different ways tasks can be related in a project.

You (and your project team) will want to construct a series of network diagrams corresponding to the number of work flow streams that you envision for your project. As with all of the work that you are producing as a project manager to date, you will want to socialize these with different team members to validate them and help build ownership of the project within the team.

Costs Revisited

With this increased clarity of you project, you can now return to the initial cost estimates you developed and refine them further. This takes you one step closer to developing your final budget.

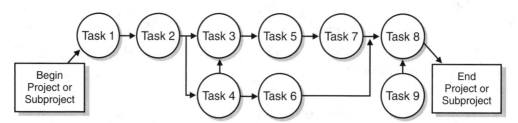

Examples of task relationships
- Task 9 is independent of Task 1
- Task 2 is a dependent task that exhibits a Start to Finish relationship with independent Task 1
- Task 4 is a dependent task that exhibits a Start to Start relationship with independent Task 3
- Task 6 is a dependent task that exhibits a Finish to Finish relationship with independent Task 7

Figure 6.7   Network Diagram Showing Task Relationships. © Copyright 2007 Pamela McGhee and Peter McAliney.

Risk Revisited

With the completion of the WBS, the Responsibility-Accountability Map, the task list, and the network diagram, you now have a clearer picture of your project. It is now time to revisit and refine the risks that were identified earlier.

With this increased understanding of the project, you can begin to better quantify the risks so that you can begin to develop contingency plans for those risks that might actually turn into realities. You can do this by assigning probabilities that the risk will occur and assign a weight to the impact the risk may have on the project. This will provide you a mechanism for determining risks that have the highest potential to negatively impact your project. Table 6.4 shows an enhanced version of the Risk Identification Chart that we developed earlier.

Note that the risks associated with Business Risk 1 (4.50), Partner Risk N (3.75), and External Risk N (3.00) present the greatest degree of risk. You would start with these three risk areas when developing risk mitigation contingency plans.

Table 6.4   Enhanced Risk Identification Chart

Risk Category	Project Risk	Probability	Probability (%)	Impact (1–10)	Weighted Impact
Project	1 . . .	M	50	2	1.00
		H	75	3	2.25
	N . . .	L	25	6	1.50
Partner	1 . . .	L	25	7	1.75
		H	75	3	2.25
	N . . .	H	75	5	3.75
Business	1 . . .	M	50	9	4.50
		M	50	5	2.50
	N . . .	M	50	2	1.00
External	1 . . .	L	25	8	2.00
		L	25	1	0.25
	N . . .	H	75	4	3.00

Note: H = High; M = Medium; L = Low. © Copyright 2007 Pamela McGhee and Peter McAliney.

TIP

Assigning probabilities has the potential to cause great concern and can be very time consuming. To simplify, for Low use a probability of 25 percent, for Medium use a probability of 50 percent, and for High use a probability of 75 percent.

Third Iteration—1,000 Feet

We now have a series of network diagrams, that when integrated, display the series of tasks, the relationships among them, and the time it will take to complete them. However, we are not yet at the level of detail we need to begin our project. We now need to develop the project schedule—who will be doing what when, for how long, and for how much. A powerful tool for developing the project schedule is the Program Evaluation Review Technique, or PERT.

Program Evaluation Review Technique

PERT was developed by the U.S. Navy to manage the Polaris Missile Program. While your project might not be as complex as that, you will find PERT is a useful tool. In decades past, the network was called a PERT Chart. We use that network as a tool to find the critical path (see Figure 6.8).

Time estimates have been assigned to the tasks in this project. In a simple example such as this, we can see by inspection that the path flowing through Tasks 1 to 2 to 4 takes 7 weeks (2 + 3 + 2) while the path flowing through Tasks 1 to 3 to 4 takes 9 weeks (2 + 5 + 2). Path 1 to 3 to 4 is the longest path of sequenced tasks that appear in this project. If there was a delay in this path (the critical path), the project would be delayed. The path represented by Tasks 1 to 2 to 4 could experience up to a two-week delay before impacting the end date of the project.

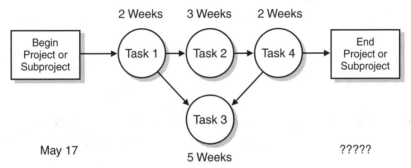

2 Weeks   3 Weeks   2 Weeks

May 17   5 Weeks   ?????

Figure 6.8   Simple Illustration of Critical Path. © Copyright 2007 Pamela McGhee and Peter McAliney.

Calculating Time Estimates

As you might notice from the previous discussion, the key to identifying the critical path is determined by the time estimates that you assign for each task. The times you assign to tasks need to be developed. But how to select the time estimates (got a dart board)?

Similar to the first way we categorized risk, we will identify not one but three time estimates:

1. *Most likely estimate (Tml):* If you had only one estimate to choose, using what you know today, this is the number you would choose?

2. *Pessimistic estimate (Tp):* If things went wrong, how long could it take?

3. *Optimistic estimate (To):* If things went right—you had the wind at your back the entire way—how long would it take?

Using these three estimates, we can come up with what we call the *expected time estimate* (*T*). This can be calculated using a simple formula:

$$\text{Task effort } (e) = \frac{4 \times \text{(Most likely estimate } (Tml)) + \text{(Most optimistic estimate } (To)) + \text{(Most pessimistic estimate } (Tp))}{6}$$

or

$$T\text{used} = \frac{(\text{Pessimistic } (Tp) + \text{Optimistic } (To) + 4 \times \text{Most likely } (Tml))}{6}$$

This formula, when used to develop a time for a single task, produces a beta curve *skewed to the right*. The results range is correct 68 percent of the time.

When the same formula is used to predict project duration, a *symmetrical* beta curve is followed (one standard deviation ± from the mean produces a results range which is correct 68 percent of the time).

You also want to obtain a measurement for the confidence you have in the estimates you developed. The amount of confidence you have in your estimates is a way to think about the risk involved in your estimates. The closer your optimistic and pessimistic estimates, the more confident you are and the less risk there is in your estimates. The greater the difference, the less confident you are and the more risk there is in your estimates. In statistics, this risk is measured by the standard deviation. For those of you who remember your statistics (not necessary), you may recall that the true estimate will be correct approximately 68 percent of the time to within one standard deviation, 95 percent of the time to within two standard deviations, and 99 percent of the time to within three standard deviations.

A simplified way to determine the standard deviation can be calculated with the following formula:

$$\text{Standard deviation} = \frac{(\text{Optimistic} - \text{Pessimistic})}{6}$$

While all of this may sound complicated, it really is not. All of this information can be calculated in a simple Excel spreadsheet. You may not want to "live and die" by the numbers that are produced, but certainly the information will provide you directional guidance for identifying those risks for which it is important to be aware.

Determining Schedule Flexibility

As noted, using a network allows us to identify critical paths (there may be more than one in any network). Another type of logic diagram, the Precedence Diagram, uses early and late starts to isolate the critical path.

Whether we use the network or the Precedence Diagram, there is the matter of float. What about the tasks that are not on the critical path? What happens if they do not get done in a timely fashion—will that slow a project down? The answer to that is maybe yes, maybe no. It depends how long they slip.

There are four dates of which a project manager need be aware when determining a project's critical path. Accordingly, he or she can redeploy resources that may be available due to the float (flexibility) in different work streams:

1. *Earliest start date (ES):* The earliest date a task can start given logic, constraints, and dependencies to other tasks.
2. *Earliest finish date (EF):* The earliest date a task can finish given logic, constraints, and dependencies to other tasks.
3. *Latest start date (LS):* The latest date a task can start before impacting the finish date of the project.
4. *Latest finish date (LF):* The latest date a task can finish before impacting the finish date of the project.

For tasks on the critical path, the late start is equal to the late finish. If the late start date is different than the late finish date, the amount of the difference is called float. Float is an important tool in that it gives the project manager leeway. If resources are needed on other parts of the project, the project manager can look to see what areas of the project have float. Resources can be shifted from these areas and redeployed in areas that need them.

However, using float does not come without risk. If the project manager uses all of the float available for a given task, that task then becomes critical. If there is a delay in completing that task, the project may be late anyway! The wise project manager is parsimonious when it comes to using float.

Knowing about networks, Precedence Diagrams, earliest-latest start, earliest-latest finish, and float, plus the concepts of task estimating when the work is unknown is key to project success. You can now use the following steps to calculate the critical path in a logic diagram and therefore calculate the time the work will take to complete, or the project time line or schedule:

1. From the WBS, select all lowest level tasks.
2. Identify dependencies and create a network or Precedence Diagram.
3. List the time estimates for each task on the network or Precedence Diagram.
4. When using a network, count up the task timings for each path. The longest path is the critical path. When using the Precedence Diagram method, use the forward and backward pass technique to isolate the critical path tasks. A critical path task is one with zero float. In this method, float equals the difference between the LS and LF for the task.
5. When using the Precedence Diagram, connect with a line all of the tasks with zero float.
6. That path is the critical path and its length represents the shortest amount of time that the work will take relative to dependencies.
7. If you have used effort time (recommended) when estimating the time a task will take to complete, then apply a conversion ratio to arrive at duration. That duration, when applied to a calendar,

Table 6.5   Simple Critical Path Analysis

Task Number	Dependent on Task Number	Time Estimate (Weeks)	Earliest Start Date	Earliest Finish Date	Latest Start Date	Latest Finish Date	Float Time (Weeks)
1	N/A	2	05-17	06-02	05-17	06-02	0
2	1	3	06-02	06-23	06-16	07-08	2
3	1	5	06-02	07-08	06-02	07-08	0
4	2, 3	2	07-08	07-22	07-08	07-22	0

© Copyright 2007 Pamela McGhee and Peter McAliney.

is your project schedule (Gantt Chart). Simply lay out the time-converted network or Precedence Diagram on a calendar. If you have made your task estimates in duration, simply layout the network or Precedence Diagram on that calendar. The good news is that any project management software will do this for you, once you have defined the task dependencies.

If we were to assign our project a start date of May 17, then the chart shown in Table 6.5 would identify our critical path.

In the example we used in Figure 6.8 on page 145, the non-critical path 1–2–4 had a float of 2 weeks (the difference between the 7 weeks it was estimated and the 9 weeks of critical path 1–3–4). The wise project manager will *not* use this float in a profligate or wasteful manner!

Budget

You have now identified all of the work and the resources required to do the work. You can revisit the budget that you have been developing as you have been adding—and socializing with other project stakeholders—detail to the work of the project. The final budget that you have put together is called the *baseline budget*. It will be this baseline budget to which all costs will be compared as you begin to work on the project.

Change Management Plan and Communication Plan

We are certain that most have heard of the old adage, "The only thing constant in life is change." When it comes to managing a project, this is acutely true. You need to develop a change management plan. The heart of the change management plan is the communications plan.

At this point, the project manager has reached out to different stakeholders in the development of the project plan. He or she now needs to reflect on all of the activity that has transpired to date and determine how communications need to be managed going forward. Mistakes will already have been made in communications—too much information, not enough information—hopefully none too bad. A key role the project manager will play during the execution of the project will be to continue to manage communications from a strategic perspective—the overall vision of the project—while keeping an eye on day-to-day operations—and changes—that may burst into the strategic perspective.

Successful project management requires managing expectations. The communications plan is the mechanism whereby all stakeholders are apprised of the project's progress. It is an important tool in managing expectations and plays a key role in the Monitoring and Controlling aspects of project management. It is the tool that will let you celebrate the victories of attaining milestones and the temporary setbacks of missed deadlines and potential overspends.

The communication plan has two elements. There is the Strategic Communications Plan and the Operating Communications Plan.

Strategic Communications Plan

The guiding principle for creating the Strategic Communications Plan is to be ready to address issues thoughtfully and in a timely fashion. We rely once again on the stakeholder analysis to help craft the Strategic Communications Plan. During the Planning stage of the project, you will need to develop the high-level outline for the

Strategic Communications Plan. Putting aside the day-to-day communications you will employ while running the project (see the Operating Communications Plan discussion that follows), one of the conversations you as a project manager need to lead is to *whom* you will communicate, *what* you will communicate to them, *how* you will communicate it to them, and how *often* you will communicate with them.

The to *Whom* is easy—Who are the stakeholders?

The *What* can be informed by an extension of your stakeholder analysis. You need to identify what issues are important for each of the stakeholders, the probability that these issues may arise, and the impact of not addressing each individual issue. What you are doing here is painting multiple pictures, or scenarios, of the future.

TIP

When building your Strategic Communications Plan, you want to be as exhaustive as possible about what issues may arise. A comprehensive exercise building your Strategic Communications Plan will help avoid potentially project-killing consequences after the project starts.

By addressing these issues in a conceptual setting—before they actually occur—you are able to see the impact of potential consequences *before* issues arise. You can use the results of this exercise to create three important project management tools—the quick shift list, the FAQ list, and the virtual file cabinet:

1. *Quick shift list:* There will be some issues that can be addressed immediately so that they will not appear as issues. Fixing them up front ameliorates the need to address them later on.
2. *FAQ list:* Some of the issues will be information-oriented. These can be directed toward single or multiple stakeholder groups. For

these, you can put together a Frequently Asked Questions (FAQ) list to circulate to the project stakeholders. This will save you from answering the same questions repeatedly and makes sure that everyone has the same answer to a question.

3. *Virtual filing cabinet:* Some issues have only the potential to occur. The virtual filing cabinet is a repository of well-thought-out solutions to a number of potential issues that may arise in the project. Doing this ahead of time, allows you to respond quickly should these issues manifest themselves. Trust us, you will have enough issues that you did not think of ahead of time to address. You want as much time to thoughtfully consider those you did not identify in advance so you can act quickly and thoughtfully on them as well. Having a virtual filing cabinet of solutions available provides you a layer of support that will turn out to be invaluable.

TIP

Many of the issues that end up in the virtual filing cabinet are of a very sensitive nature. You will want to consult with the appropriate individuals in the organization when you put together the responses for issues that end up in the virtual filing cabinet.

The *How* you will communicate to them is another decision that you want to make and share with stakeholders during this last stage of the planning phase of the project. Some stakeholders only need to be apprised in person at key milestones while others need more personal contact on an ongoing basis—you will want to learn early the preferred medium and frequency that different stakeholders want. You will want to look at how to employ such communication mechanisms as town hall meetings, departmental visits, e-mails, project meetings, memos, or podcasts.

Special care needs to be taken in the communications plan as it relates to the client stakeholders. Chances are the project you are working on will be upsetting to the way they have been doing their work or conducting business so there will be some element of fear, uncertainty, and doubt that they will be experiencing. More personal contact may be required at different phases of the project to assure the clients that, if applicable, you are available to help them through any changes they may need to make in order to accept your project deliverables.

Last, you want to think about the *How Often*. As mentioned, some of the stakeholders will not need too much contact, while others will. Additionally, this may change during different phases of the project. Thinking through this ahead of time is an important part of the Strategic Communications Plan. In Table 6.6 we illustrate some elements that should be embodied in the Strategic Communications Plan.

Operating Communications Plan

The Operating Communications Plan is the plan addressing how day-to-day communications will occur among the project team, clients, vendors, and, to a lesser extent, company managers. This is the set of management routines, meetings, checkpoints, milestones, and audits that occur as the project unfolds.

This, too, needs to be revisited from time to time as the project progresses. For example, during Project Concept, two individuals may be driving the output of a particular work step and are applied to the project for 100 percent of their time. At a later point in the project—in the Planning stage, for example—they may be much less than fully applied to the project. The Operating Communications Plan should acknowledge this by answering the following questions:

- To what extent do these individuals need to come to project meetings?
- What is the level of project detail of which they must be kept apprised?

Table 6.6 Stakeholder Chart—Strategic Communications Plan

Stakeholder Group	Individual	Potential Issues	Probability Issues May Arise
Project team	Person A		
	Person B		
	…		
	Person X		
Customer	Key contact A		
	Key contact B		
	…		
	Key contact X		
Sponsor	Sponsor A		
	Sponsor B		
	…		
	Sponsor X		
Company managers	Functional		
	Geographical		
	…		
	Manager X		
Vendors/suppliers	Vendor A		
	Vendor B		
	…		
	Vendor X		

Impact of Not Addressing Issue	Response to Potential Issue	How Often to Communicate	How to Communicate

- How do you obtain specific portions of their time when they move on to other projects?
- What input will you provide for their overall performance review?

Risk Analysis and Contingency Plans

You want to revisit the risk analysis that you have been diligently building as you are bringing your project plan to a close. Have you learned anything that might change the risk probabilities that you assigned earlier? Have you learned anything that will change the impact to the project associated with risks? Are the contingency plans that you have started to create adequate to address your perceived risks?

Before you get the final sign-off to begin the project, you will want to review the risk management plan, with the corresponding contingency plans, and address any deficiencies that might exist.

Quality Plan

A project manager should not make assumptions around quality. In the Charter, certain standards around quality were articulated. But like the other elements of the Project Plan, they were more theoretical in the Charter than they are now that additional detail has been developed. The project manager needs to rearticulate the quality policy of the project:

- *Standards:* What are general acceptance levels of completed deliverables? How do they relate to company and industry standards?
- *Cost of quality:* What cost will be incurred to assure quality? Who will bear the cost to ensure quality within the project?
- *Intervention policy:* What recourse does the project manager have to address quality issues inside the project? Outside the project?

The project manager needs to create an enhanced quality policy document to include within the project plan. This policy needs to be circulated and socialized with the project's stakeholders. This will become a very important tool for helping manage expectations around the project.

Project Sign-Off

All the pieces are assembled. They have been socialized among different project stakeholders. The project manager needs to put together a final package and receive sign-offs from the appropriate stakeholders. The package should include the following items:

- Charter
- WBS
- Network diagram
- Precedence Diagram
- Project schedule (Gantt Chart)
- Change Management and Communications Plan
- Stakeholder analysis
- Budget
- Quality Plan
- Risk Analysis and Contingency Plans

Conclusion

At this point you might be saying to yourself, "Whew! That was a lot of work!" But remember where you were at the beginning of this chapter.

Yes, you did pull much together in this chapter. With all of the preceding done, you are now ready to . . .

REAL LIFE EXPERIENCES FROM THE TRENCHES

VIGNETTE 6—Project Management: A Behavioral Approach That Requires Discipline

In the early 1990s, the Research Development & Engineering (RD&E) center for a major international metals producer began an intense effort to develop a series of quality-related metrics that could be used to measure the overall performance of that center in its development of new metal products and metal-producing processes for its business unit clients. In this initiative, the client-driven, quality-metrics project team surveyed many of the business unit leaders (the clients for the RD&E center's technical development efforts) to identify what the expectations of this leadership group were for the RD&E center related to how the technical staff at the center completed its work. The survey (in which over 600 people participated) did not deal with the content of the research—but rather the *how* or the processes that the RD&E center used to conduct its work for its business unit clients.

The overwhelming message that the business unit leadership conveyed was that they simply wanted "what had been promised to be delivered on time and within budget." From this particular initiative, the center derived a series of client-driven, quality metrics the RD&E center management used as the tools to measure one dimension of the overall center's performance. The key client-driven metric that the center adopted was "percent of deliverables delivered." For each RD&E program, the project leader developed in concert with the business unit clients a statement of the key deliverables that each RD&E program was to deliver by the end of the funding year.

While valuable to the RD&E center management and to its business unit clients, the specific measure, however, did not address the root cause or the reasons for this measure being adopted to begin with. This failure laid with the center's failure or inability to use project management in an effective manner in conducting its RD&E activities.

The RD&E center only began to address this root cause during its reengineering effort that occurred several years after the client-driven quality metrics initiative. During this latter initiative, another project team—the reengineering team—collected sufficient data to begin to understand that the root cause behind the "percent deliverables delivered" measure was the lack of project management—skills, discipline, tools, and so on—within the research community. Their data indicated that deadlines were missed and project schedules were routinely not followed. While the deliverables metric was being used to measure the center's performance, adequate cultural changes—akin to a disciplined approach to RD&E—had not yet occurred.

A key recommendation that the reengineering project team made was to instill a rigorous project management culture within the RD&E center. The RD&E leadership team adopted this recommendation and created a Project Management Office under the leadership of one of the center's respected division managers.

The intent of that office was twofold:

1. Provide training to the R&D project leaders to enhance their skills in managing projects—both one-on-one and group training efforts.
2. Provide project management leadership for a few highly visible projects with these projects reporting to the head of the Project Management Office (PMO).

Post Script: Creating a project management culture requires great discipline. In this company's case, those in the organization outside the RD&E department had not adopted the project management mindset. This was evidenced when the company imposed across the board budget cuts. The center's management team determined that the Project Management Office could not be sustained due to the loss in RD&E budget dollars. The Project Management Office was closed and PMO head took early retirement. Unfortunately, the RD&E center reverted back to an environment of frustration and missed deadlines.

A. ROBERT WASSON
Toffler Associates

CHAPTER 7

Status Reporting: What to Tell, When, and to Whom

The phrase that anyone associated with a project loves to hear is that the project is "on time and on budget." Even more magical is when you hear that a project is "ahead of schedule and under budget." What does that really mean, though, and how do you get to that place?

As we have acknowledged, a project consists of many moving and interrelated parts. These interrelationships span work activities, super sets of work activities, and the different stakeholders associated with the project. In order to make sure the project moves toward its intended goal, the project manager needs to be like a traffic officer at a very busy intersection, identifying and prioritizing the flow of information throughout the project and among its participants. He or she must make judgments on what information is important and what information is not important. Information that is deemed important must be delivered quickly. Some information—either because it is unimportant or incomplete without an explanation—has the potential to distract the project's players and can lead to unintended, negative consequences. The project manager cannot discount this information out of hand, but rather will have to exhibit his or her professional business judgment on how best to handle it.

A project manager is responsible and accountable to the project sponsor, project resources, and other project stakeholders on three dimensions associated with a project's progress: planned versus actual progress, changes in the project, and potential and/or actual project disruption.

Before addressing these three dimensions of project progress, however, we briefly address communications mechanisms available to the project manager. We have at our disposal a very powerful, top-level reporting tool—the *Elevator Report.*

Communications Mechanisms

The following chapter addresses in more detail the Strategic Communication Plan and the Operating Communication Plan. However, the project manager has to have an understanding of the communications mechanisms that she has in her communications toolbox. A knowledge of these communication mechanisms—e-mail, phone, and in-person communications—and more importantly, how and when to use them, will be essential in communicating all facets of the project. Table 7.1 provides a summary of these mechanisms and some guidelines on when to use them.

TIP

While e-mail is a powerful communications mechanism, do not over rely on it. For those aspects of communication that require a timely response, either pick up the phone or drop by the stakeholder's office if convenient.

The Elevator Report

Because of all the moving parts involved in a project, it is nearly impossible for a project manager to have all of the information related

Table 7.1   Communications Mechanisms

E-Mail	Phone	In Person
Communicate quickly and concisely.	Access someone conveniently (cell phones).	Reduce potential for miscommunications.
Share information without interrupting the recipient.	Explain subject in further detail.	For sensitive and important topics.
Have a record of shared information for future use.	Communicate when Internet or face-to-face unavailable.	Convey message with "complete" communication (body language, voice inflection, facial expression).
Share a message 24/7.	Receive an immediate response.	Build relationship and develop rapport.
Save money on postage.		
Easier than fax or mail.		
Share a message with many.		

© Copyright 2007 Pamela McGhee and Peter McAliney.

to the project at his or her finger tips at all times. However, he or she should be able to provide the project sponsor or client a snapshot of key activities at any point in time in a simple and concise delivery. And what is it that the sponsor or client usually wants to know in either a formal setting (i.e., a status report meeting) or in an informal setting (i.e., chance hallway meeting)?

The Sponsor, stakeholders, and clients want to know what was accomplished this period, what they have to look forward to completing in the near future, and what issues exist that could negatively impact the project. We call this the "Elevator Report." Just as an entrepreneur needs to be able to pitch his or her idea in the space of time it takes to go 20 floors in an elevator, the entrepreneurial project manager needs to be able to concisely report on his or her project to stakeholders when they ask. Whether delivering information on the project in an e-mail, on the phone, or in person, the project manager needs to carefully navigate the ground between too much information and too little information. Additionally, the project manager is expected to deliver a crisp analysis of the current state of his or her project. Doing so will add to the credibility of the project manager as well as add to the credibility of the project itself.

Table 7.2 (on pp. 166–169) outlines a template for a common status report called the *Elevator Report* that can be used to report high-level project status. In the following sections, we describe how to find the information to complete this powerful report. For now, though, it is important to understand how to present this information to satisfy the information needs of project stakeholders.

The elements of the Elevator Report are:

- *Activity category:* These represent either accomplishments or issues.

   Accomplishments are reported at two levels:

1. *Completed this period:* Major activities completed in current period.
2. *Scheduled for completion in upcoming period:* Due for completion in upcoming period.

   Issues are reported at three levels:

1. *Closed this period:* A prior issue that was resolved during the current period.
2. *Open from prior period:* A prior issue that remains open from a prior period.
3. *Opened in current period:* A newly identified issue that warrants the attention of the project manager.

- *Completion status:* Status of the accomplishment or issue.
   For accomplishments:

   —*Ahead or behind schedule:* Whether the accomplishment that was completed finished ahead, on, or behind the scheduled date.

—Ahead or behind budget: Whether the accomplishment that was completed finished ahead, on, or behind the scheduled budget.

—Date closed: Date accomplishment was completed.

   For issues:

—Date reported: When issue was first identified.

—Date due: Planned resolution date of the issue.

—Date closed: Actual resolution date of the issue.

- *Critical path:* Does this accomplishment or issue appear on the critical path? If so, it carries more weight and, if an issue, may require the application of more resources to complete.
- *Stakeholders directly impacted:* Which stakeholders are impacted by this accomplishment or issue. Depending on the potential impact to the project, you may need to contact them and proactively manage the situation.

TIP

This Elevator Report can very easily be housed in an Excel spreadsheet. Sorting by stakeholder will allow you to give personalized reports to stakeholders that directly address their interest areas without burdening them with areas that do not interest them.

- *Accomplishment/Issue:* What the nature of the accomplishment or issue is.
- *Notes:* Any additional, clarifying information that will help you better explain the accomplishment or the issue.
- *Responsible party:* The name of the individual(s) who are responsible for the accomplishment or the issue. Don't forget to celebrate success when accomplishments occur during a project—this can add significantly to team morale and in building confidence among other stakeholders.

Table 7.2 Elevator Report

Prepared by: _____				
Completion Status				
Activity Category	Ahead/ On/Behind Schedule	Ahead/ On/Behind Budget	Date Close	Critical Path (Y/N)
Significant accomplishments for current period				
Significant accomplishments for upcoming period				

Date: _____			
Stakeholders Directly Impacted	Accomplishment	Notes	Responsible

(continued)

Table 7.2 *(Continued)*

Completion Status				
Activity Category	Date Reported	Date Due	Date Close	Critical Path (Y/N)
Open issues closed from prior period				
Open issues Remaining from prior period			Open	
			Open	
			Open	
			Open	
			Open	
			Open	
New issues added for current period			Open	
			Open	
			Open	
			Open	
			Open	
			Open	

Stakeholders Directly Impacted	Issue	Notes	Responsible

There are many off-the-shelf project management software packages that you can use to track in detail all of the project activities, milestones, critical paths, and other time and budget considerations associated with a project. Type "project management software" into a search engine on your computer and you will receive a surfeit of product offerings. Some are even "open source" (free or at a nominal charge).

Planned Progress

Wouldn't it be nice if everyone shook hands when the Charter and Project Plan were established and agreed to meet at the end date of the project to celebrate the project's success?

Well, this would mean living in a world of no surprises, no changes, no risks, no unanticipated events, and the project manager having the ability to predict the future!

We don't live in such a world.

So, one of the *key* roles of a project manager is to communicate the ordinary progress of the project and any extraordinary circumstances the project may run into during the life of the project. This section addresses tracking the *ordinary* progress of the project.

Time Line and Budget Revisited

To begin to think about the project's progress—and how a project manager needs to report the project's progress—we need to refer back to the time line and the budget that was originally put together in the planning stages of the project. Recalling that both of these represent a contract that the stakeholders agreed to when the project was launched (the time line for delivery dates and the budget for monetary commitments), these play an instrumental role in managing stakeholders' expectations. As such, both the time line and the budget provide the basis for which all current work activity must be compared. As we all have heard many times over, "Time is Money." Hence, when we are reporting on a project's progress, we need to think about reporting it in terms of time and money.

Progress as It Relates to the Time Line

All projects are driven by time, whether it is a primary driver or a secondary driver. To think of time as a primary driver, think of a building developer who is trying to complete a project so families can move in before a September school start or an IT project manager who needs to get a system online before a specified calendar date to accommodate a mandated compliance change. Other projects are not driven by time. To think of time as a secondary driver, think of that same building developer who is completing a project only as he or she has extra resources available as surplus from other projects that he or she has underway or an IT project manager implementing a discretionary IT system that has low priority in an organization. Whatever role time plays in the completion of the project, a project manager needs to be able to report the status of a project to his or her stakeholders in terms of how the project is progressing.

Progress as It Relates to Budget

Projects also generate a series of indirect and/or direct costs. The cash needs of a project are often called the *burn rate* of the project. That is, at what rate does the project require, or "burn," cash to move forward. It is important to recognize that the burn rate of the project is not necessarily constant throughout the life of the project. In the Planning stage, the project manager provided a pro forma cash needs analysis to accommodate the cash needs of the project. As the project progresses, the project manager must keep his or her financial stakeholder group cognizant of the burn rate so that funding the project is aligned with the overall cash needs of the organization.

Some direct costs associated with projects are in-house labor costs, overtime costs, contractor costs, and procurement costs of materials and supplies. Some indirect costs associated with projects are supervisory costs, redundancy costs, and opportunity costs.

TIP

Project tracking software will track time and budget considerations down to a very small unit level. The successful project manager will be able to sort through this detail to make sure the right items end up on the Elevator Report.

Tracking Tools to Determine What's Important

The question becomes what to put on the Elevator Report. There are a number of tools the project manager has available to him to help put an elevator report together that will be meaningful and have significant impact:

- *Variance analysis:* The variance analysis is a simple tool that allows you to compare actual progress with anticipated progress as outlined in the budget. The project manager can use it to compare actual budget, schedule, and quality with targets. In Figure 7.1, we can see that Activity B is suffering a larger negative variance than Activity A. All things being equal (i.e., both are—or are not— on the critical path), the astute project manager will be looking to better understand what is happening with both activities that are falling behind. However, in an environment of constrained resources, he or she would probably look to apply additional resources to Activity B before Activity A.

- *Trend analysis:* Trend analysis looks to see if the progress is getting better, worse, or staying the same. This also can be used to track progress against budget, schedule, and quality with targets.

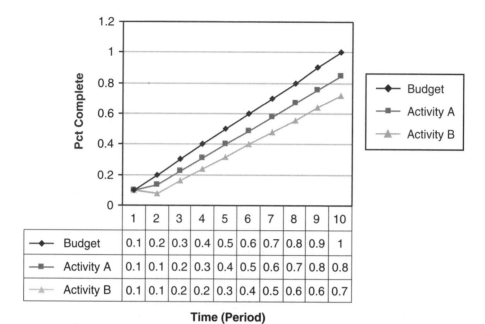

		1	2	3	4	5	6	7	8	9	10
◆	Budget	0.1	0.2	0.3	0.4	0.5	0.6	0.7	0.8	0.9	1
■	Activity A	0.1	0.1	0.2	0.3	0.4	0.5	0.6	0.7	0.8	0.8
▲	Activity B	0.1	0.1	0.2	0.2	0.3	0.4	0.5	0.6	0.6	0.7

Time (Period)

Figure 7.1 Activity Completion—Variance Analysis. © Copyright 2007 Pamela McGhee and Peter McAliney.

In Figure 7.2, we see that although both Activity A and Activity B are off budget, a corrective action applied to Activity B in period 5 (as suggested through the use of the variance analysis in Figure 7.1) shows that Activity B is improving and that perhaps attention now needs to be applied to Activity A.

- *Earned Value Analysis (EVA):* A more sophisticated tool used to track and support a project's progress is the EVA. While variance analysis and trend analysis provide high-level direction in determining a project's performance, EVA calculates cost, scheduling, and scope measurements together to determine productivity indices, performance measurements, as well as more refined variances of schedule and budget. EVA reports on such measurements as:

1. Budgeted Cost of Work Scheduled (BCWS): Also called the planned value, this is what appears in your original budget.

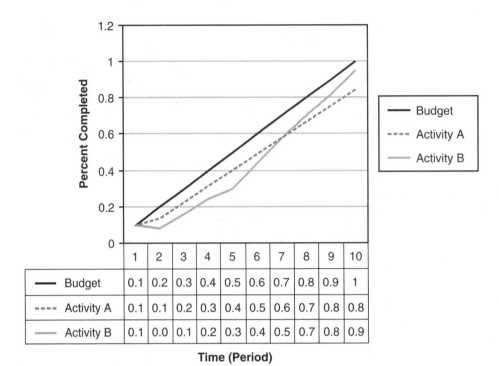

Time (Period)	1	2	3	4	5	6	7	8	9	10
——— Budget	0.1	0.2	0.3	0.4	0.5	0.6	0.7	0.8	0.9	1
---- Activity A	0.1	0.1	0.2	0.3	0.4	0.5	0.6	0.7	0.8	0.8
——— Activity B	0.1	0.0	0.1	0.2	0.3	0.4	0.5	0.7	0.8	0.9

Time (Period)

Figure 7.2   Activity Completion—Trend Analysis. © Copyright 2007 Pamela McGhee and Peter McAliney.

How much do you think the project will cost? The BCWS at the end of a project is called the Budget at Completion, or BAC.

2. Actual Cost of Work Performed (ACWP): Also called the actual cost, this tracks costs as they are actually incurred on the project.

3. Budget Cost of Work Performed (BCWP): Also called the earned value, this looks at the work that was performed (for which you paid actual money) and reports what the original budget was for this work. If the project is on time and on budget, then this should equal the BCWS.

Using these three concepts, we can accurately track a project's schedule and budget to develop schedule variances (and a scheduling index) and cost variances (and a cost index):

- *Schedule Variance (SV) and Schedule Variance Index (SVI):* The SV and SVI compare the amount of money scheduled to be spent on a project (or the project to some point in time) with the amount of work that was paid for and actually accomplished. The SV and SVI can be used to help the project manager predict how much time it will take to finish the project.

  This can be reported either in absolute terms (SV) or as an index (SVI) and can be calculated from the concepts described previously:

$$SV = BCWP - BCWS$$

  While it is not necessary to memorize the formulas, you do want to remember that bad SV variances are negative and good variances are positive. Similarly, bad SVI variances are less than one and good SVI variances are greater than one.

- *Cost Variance (CV) and Cost Variance Index (CVI):* The CV and CVI compare the amount of money actually spent on a project (or the project to some point in time) with the amount of work that was paid for and actually accomplished. The CV and CVI can be used to help the project manager predict how much money it will take to finish the project.

  This can be reported either in absolute terms (CV) or as an index (CVI) and can be calculated from the concepts described previously:

$$CV = BCWP - ACWP$$

$$CVI = \frac{BCWP}{ACWP}$$

  While it is not necessary to memorize these formulas either, you do want to remember that bad CV variances are negative and good variances are positive. Similarly, bad CVI variances are less than one and good CVI variances are greater than one.

Other information that you will want to have readily available to you is what percent complete you are at any given point in time and what percent of the originally allocated money has been spent to date. These two questions often come from your project sponsor who is thinking about your project from a wider perspective and is not always privy to the day-to-day details of the project like you are.

These, too, are easy to develop within the earned value framework:

- *Percent complete:* Quite simply, how far along in the project you are:

$$\text{Percent complete} = \frac{\text{BCWP}}{\text{BAC}}$$

- *Percent spent:* Quite simply, how much money you have already spent of the originally allocated budget.

$$\text{Percent spent} = \frac{\text{ACWP}}{\text{BAC}}$$

Project Changes

A project travels through many twists and turns before it is completed. While one cannot predict the nature of specific changes that may be required to bring a project to completion, one can state with a pretty high degree of certainty that changes will occur. The important thing to plan for, as a project manager, is that a process is in place to recognize and act upon any changes that emerge as the project progresses. And, more importantly, this process should be shared with all project stakeholders well in advance of the first time a change is required.

TIP

It is important to recognize as early as possible that a change may be impending. A good project manager will manage stakeholder expectations as they relate to the change request process so that changes are dealt with

sooner when there is time to explore options rather than later when changes can quickly turn into a project crisis.

While all change requests should flow through the project manager, some projects have an additional governing board that oversees the project. This body goes by many names, such as Change Review Board, Change Control Board, Project Review Board, and Change Board. For an organization that is managing many projects concurrently, this body may come out of the office of project management (Project Management Office or PMO). This makes sense because the office of project management has visibility across many projects and can determine the impact of the change for not only the individual projects, but for all projects across the organization. If an organization has this governing body, the project manager must recognize this as a very important stakeholder group that needs to be managed.

A project manager needs to make sure he or she creates and socializes the Change Process with the stakeholders when the project is launched. Figure 7.3 displays a sample Change Request Process. The important thing to notice about this process is that even when a change request is denied, it is the project manager's responsibility to inform the original requestor with the reasoning behind the

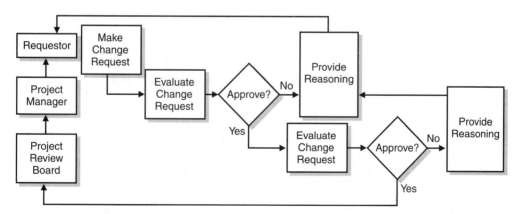

Figure 7.3 Change Request Process. © Copyright 2007 Pamela McGhee and Peter McAliney.

denied request. This information will help the requestor put the original change request within not only the project with which he or she is associated, but also within the context of the entire organization. This additional context will enhance the individual project by helping individuals recommit to the purpose of their project within the overall goals of the organizations.

Equally important to having a well-articulated change review process, a project manager needs to put together a standard Change Request Form. This form serves two purposes:

1. The instrument for creating a single point of communication around changes requested for a project, and
2. A document to include in the permanent record of the project to document the project audit trail.

A sample Change Request Form is shown in Table 7.3 (on pp. 180–181).

Not all changes are created equal. Some may be only minor course corrections (i.e., changing out a nonessential vendor), while others have the potential to impact the scope of the project. For those changes impacting the scope of the project, the project manager needs to make sure they update the Charter and track the change in the Project Charter's Revision Log.

Project Disruptions—Risk Happens

There are changes and then there are disruptions. Hopefully, you have identified the potential disruptions in your risk management plan, recalling that they can come from four key areas:

1. Project related risks
2. Partner related risks

3. Business related risks
4. External related risks

The most important thing a project manager needs to do in the face of a major disruption is to *stay calm.* All eyes are on a project manager when a major disruption occurs and the project's success will depend on how a project manager responds to a major project disruption. It is important to assure all stakeholder groups that the situation is being managed. Loss of confidence by any stakeholder group can have a severe impact on the ability of a project and project manager to respond to the specific project disruption.

After suffering the expected discouragement when the project disruption first manifests itself, the good project manager will swing immediately into action mode. He or she has a number of strategies available for dealing with risk:

- *Suffer it:* Don't do anything and see how events play out. This does not mean ignoring it, but rather not immediately moving into an action mode.

- *Prevention:* Or avoidance, means that you would have taken preventive measures to make sure the risk does not occur.

- *Transference:* Shift the risk to someone else. Your risk plan may have called for purchasing an insurance policy or obtaining specific wording in a contract that would transfer the risk in the event that it occurred.

- *Mitigating:* Reduce the potential impact of the risk.

- *Addressing:* When all else fails, you have to address the risk. This entails embarking into problem-solving mode and pulling the team together to collectively brainstorm ideas that will work the project around the disruption. Team-driven root cause analysis is an effective tool at the project manager's disposal to help them

Table 7.3   Change Request Form

Project Name _____	Change Tracking No. _____

Requestor name _____
Contact info _____
Date requested _____

Approved (Y/N)   Date approved _____

_____

To be completed by requestor
Description of change _____
_____

Reason for change _____
_____

Anticipated impact to project if change not undertaken _____
_____
_____

Anticipated impact to other parts of project if change is made _____
_____
_____

Alternatives to undertake if change is not possible _____
_____
_____

Estimated additional time and cost to effect change _____
_____
_____
_____

Table 7.3 *(Continued)*

Estimated additional time and cost to effect change _____

_____

_____

_____

_____

To be completed by project manager
Relevant comments on: _____
• Not undertaking change   _____
• Impact to other parts   _____
• Alternatives   _____
                                         _____
                                         _____
                                         _____
                                         _____
                                         _____
                                         _____

Recommendation to Change Board _____

_____

_____

To be completed by Change Board

Decision _____

_____

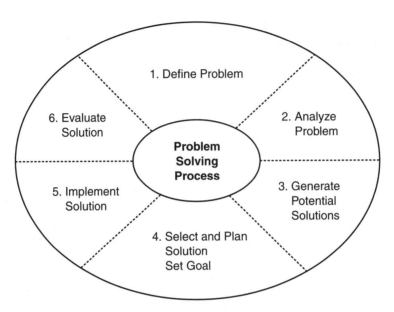

Figure 7.4   Oval within Oval Problem-Solving Tool. © Copyright 2007 Pamela McGhee and Peter McAliney.

resolve a major project disruption. In Figure 7.4 we illustrate a model problem-solving tool that can help a project manager and his or her team come up with solutions to even the most major project disruptions in an organized and auditable fashion.

Project disruptions are part of "a day in the life" for any project manager. The successful project manager will rise to the occasion and meet these disruptions head on.

Reporting Quality

You will have to assure your stakeholders that the work being done on the project is meeting the standards as defined in the Quality Plan that was developed. While there are many ways of enforcing quality, the P-D-C-A cycle, as described by Edward Deming as part of Total Quality

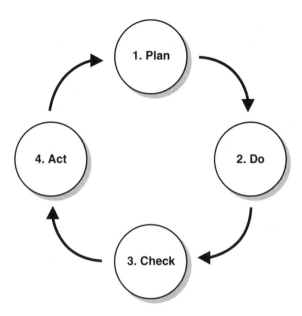

Figure 7.5   The P-D-C-A Cycle. © Copyright 2007 Pamela McGhee and Peter McAliney.

Management, is a useful tool for enforcing quality during the work of the project. In Figure 7.5 we show the classic P-D-C-A cycle that you will probably want to employ while managing a project. The Risk Analysis chart will inform you where you should apply it—look to those areas of the project that continue to exhibit an element of high risk.

Proactively reporting to project stakeholders results in assuring them that you are committed to the quality standards articulated in the project plan.

Reporting Project Completion

Upon successful completion of a project, the first thing that comes to mind for (most) project managers is to celebrate success by popping a cork on his or her favorite bubbly. Go ahead—it is well deserved. However, after the mandatory team celebrations, there are still some important loose ends that need to be completed. But what does *successful completion* mean? This term needs to be agreed upon by all stakeholders and it is the project manager's job to make sure a completed project means "successful" completion for all stakeholders. And when is this—when all stakeholders agree that it is finished.

Upon completion of a project, the project manager is responsible for making sure a number of essential items are addressed. These include:

- Client/sponsor/stakeholder sign-offs
- Accounting close
- Contracts close
- Lessons learned document
  —Content lessons
  —Process improvement lessons
- Project documentation archival
- Project performance appraisals

Organizations should benefit from a well-run project. All too many projects end up getting filed into oblivion, never to be seen or heard of again. You should take it upon yourself as a project manager to make sure any lessons learned that can benefit the organization are documented to help the organization in future project endeavors.

By completing all of the preceding activities, both the individuals who participated on the project and the organization as a whole gets to benefit from a well run, successful product.

New Technologies: Dashboards and Blogs

The concept of a *dashboard*—a concise representation of key indicators—can be applied to project management as well. With open access software readily available one could easily construct a dashboard that houses all of the information that is important to a project. This dashboard should follow the same guidelines as the Elevator Report—not too much, not too little. As a more visually appealing representation, It can be used to either complement or replace the Elevator Report.

It is worth mentioning, also, the concept of blogging (i.e., web logs). Project managers could establish an additional avenue of communication that is housed in a blog. This way, stakeholders can check in and out at their convenience to see what is happening with a project. Specific areas can be established that are of interest to individuals across stakeholder groups. In using blogs, the project manager can open up a dialogue that helps to build team spirit and camaraderie. The blogs can also serve as fertile ground for solving—or preventing—problems along the way. And, oh yes, blogging can also be used to plan team extracurricular activities as well.

Conclusion

A project manager needs to know all of the intimate details of a project. At the same time, he or she must be able to sort through the myriad details and provide meaningful information to different stakeholders as the project progresses. The information that a project manager reports on can be everything from ongoing work activities, completed milestones, changes, delays, major interruptions, and a host of other project-related details. The project manager has many tools available to him or her, including different communications mechanisms, reports, statistical methods, and problem-solving tools.

REAL LIFE EXPERIENCES FROM THE TRENCHES

VIGNETTE 7—The Wisdom in Waiting

I was working in the medical applications group of a large data storage manufacturer. One of the value-added resellers (VARs) we were working with had secured a contract to implement a comprehensive medical application (i.e., financials, clinical analysis, laboratory) into a regional hospital and I was asked to be on the project team to represent the data storage component of the solution. The application required many computer servers and a large storage access network (SAN) storage fiber network. The solution was to be a client/server-based application that would replace the existing configuration of terminals with personal computers.

The IT manager at the regional hospital was the project manager for the implementation of this new system. The team consisted of the VAR, me, representatives from two other hardware/software providers, the client (the hospital's area managers), and the IT group. The specific members of the IT group she was assigned at the hospital were a relatively inexperienced and young team, but all very technically proficient. She had worked with the team to develop a Project Charter and reporting system to manage the project. Upon acceptance of the Project Charter, we were off and running.

Somewhere along the way, the system architects in the IT group at the client hospital site started moving in a direction away from that specified in the Project Charter. They started to design a solution that was much more technical than originally planned for (as articulated in the Charter), budgeted, or needed. The IT staff at the client site felt that since they had the budget and the go ahead to implement this large medical application, it was theirs to "own" as it related to the development of the system. As members of the IT group learned more about the latest technology available from my company and providers of other hardware for the computer room, they started layering more and more advanced technology into the system design. From what limited view I had, I saw that this additional technology really added little or nothing to the end user environment. I was not sure where the IT department was going, so I put this information away in my "yellow flag" file to closely monitor.

The system's client at the client hospital site—the area managers—however, became concerned as well. When an interview by the IT department took a turn toward the ultra-technical, and the area managers started answering questions about technical needs that they knew for sure they did not have, they became concerned. After the interview, a representative of the area managers followed up with the IT manager. The IT manager checked with me and I expressed the same concerns as the client. The IT manager realized immediately that the IT group focus had to be redirected.

Rather than confront the IT technical staff, the IT manager instructed them to shadow hospital workers to understand their jobs and the requirements. In this way, the IT technical staff would see firsthand what the true system and other equipment requirements were. After this exercise, the IT technical staff came back with a solution that was more in line with the original system requirements. The project manager debriefed the team when they returned. Together, they "discovered" the potential misdirection and quickly redirected the project. The IT manager did not have to resort to chastising the staff for making a wrong turn, but rather gave them the opportunity to correct their own missteps—without losing credibility.

To make sure this did not occur again, the IT manager inserted additional checkpoints into the project process.

Hospital group meetings were held on a more frequent basis to validate findings and get the end user to buy in before moving forward.

I took a lot away from that experience. From my perspective as a team member, I have a management responsibility as well. I could have gone to the IT manager with my concern right away. Instead, because I was a peripheral player, I chose to wait to see if a more significant player would raise the issue—you always want to make sure you understand and respect the "chain of command" as it relates to noncritical issues. In this case, I did not see these early missteps as critical (yet) and waited to see if the natural course of events would play out. In this case, they did and the situation was resolved when the area managers brought this issue to the project manager's attention. However, at some point, if the condition persisted, it would have been my job to make the project manager aware of what was going on.

From the IT manager's perspective, she had a number of different ways to handle the "wrong turn" that the inexperienced, technically awed IT staff had made. She chose to give them the opportunity to recognize their own mistake. She did not put them in a position whereby they lost credibility with their clients. Instead, they resolved the problem on their own and as a result of the experience, they emerged as stronger professionals.

P.S. Oh, by the way, the project ended on time and on budget.

DEBORAH Z. FARMER
J. J. Wild

CHAPTER 8

The Management Part of Project Management

Simply stated, it is the project manager's responsibility to make sure that the project is delivered—period.

So far, we have focused pretty pointedly on the technical aspects of project management. One of the primary keys to the success of a project, however, is not technical. It is, rather, the way that all of the individuals associated with the project work together toward the common goal of getting the project completed. Not only as a project manager must you juggle all of the ongoing work, but in addition to that you have to manage all of the people-related issues that are involved when you get any group of individuals together. That can prove to be very challenging.

You have been put in charge of a project. Now what? You have proven that you are very good at what you do—that's why you have been chosen to lead the project. But chances are that the skills required for your technical work are only a partial list of those skills required to be an effective project manager.

TIP

Look at every project management assignment as a professional development opportunity. Identify skills that you want to develop during the course of leading your project to success.

You have the dual challenge of not only leading a successful project (which benefits the organization), but also the opportunity to develop your own professional skill set (which benefits you and your career). Yes, we all know the textbook definition of management as planning, organizing, leading, and controlling (if unfamiliar with these concepts, pick up any basic management textbook). However, what does this mean as it relates to *project* management?

Skills and Qualities Required of a Project Manager

A good project manager needs to exhibit a number of skills and qualities. While you probably have developed most (if not all) of these skills and qualities, you will want to identify two or three that you want to develop further during the course of the project. For example, these skills and qualities might include:

- *Visionary leadership:* Project team members, clients, and end customers will develop confidence in a successful project outcome when it is lead by a project manager who can create, communicate, and live a project's vision. A project leader with vision will help all those associated with the project feel ownership in the process of bringing the project to life and the delivery of the project's finished product.

- *Communication:* There are a number of roles associated with a project. Each role has a corresponding portfolio of information that it needs and shares with others associated with the project. Managing the communication of this information through the network of relationships, while at times can be challenging, is a very important activity that needs to occur. A project manager needs to be able to communicate with people on the project delivery team, the clients, and many others both within and outside of the organization (e.g., suppliers, industry and user groups, and government entities). He or she needs to articulate clearly the needs of the project as it relates to the project's goals, individual and group responsibilities, and performance expectations. He or she needs to be able to communicate clearly both positive (the easy part) and negative (the not-so-easy part) feedback to make sure the project stays on track. The successful project manager will have a strong command of both written and oral communications.

- *Negotiation:* Negotiating skills are important to secure and retain project resources. The successful project manager needs to make sure he or she maintains the proper perspective about his or her project. It is very easy to think that the sun will not rise or set based on the outcome of an individual project, but the good project manager must recognize the need to complete that project within the larger organizational perspective. While some have a more natural aptitude toward negotiating, negotiating itself is made much easier when the project manager has developed and articulated a strong vision around the project itself.

- *Problem solving:* You can be sure you will encounter myriad problems on your project. Some you will have seen before, some not. Some that are easy, some not. Some that you will need to solve by yourself, some where you can reach out to either your team or other trusted colleagues not involved with the project. Given the range of problems you will encounter, you will need to be able to sort through the problems that arise and determine the potential impact of that problem. The Problem-Solving

Impact Tool illustrated in Figure 8.1 is a simple decision tree that offers you a quick way to sort and prioritize problems as they arise.

- *Integrity:* As project manager, you are under many microscopes—team members, clients, stakeholders—your behavior will set the ethical tone for the project. You will be judged by your actions, not your words. You will find yourself in many tight spots along the way, but you need to always remember that a small compromise to your integrity in the short term may tarnish your overall integrity as project manager in the long run. Follow the *New York Times* rule—if you do not want to see your action on the front page of the *New York Times,* then you probably should not do it!

- *Calm under pressure:* There will be plenty of occasions when you will need to exhibit calm under pressure. Your actions are viewed under those microscopes, so it is important to give the appearance that you are on top of the situation (even when you are not!).

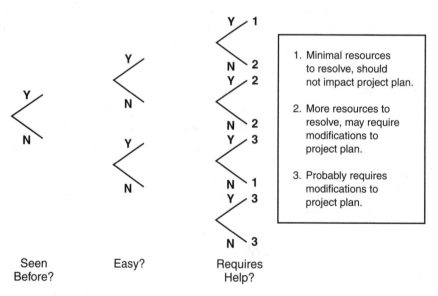

Figure 8.1   Project-Solving Impact Tool. © Copyright 2007 Pamela McGhee and Peter McAliney.

Avoid knee-jerk reactions, especially the quick e-mail dashed off clouded in an emotional fog. Sometimes—if the situation allows—you will want to apply the "24-hour rule," which, simply stated, means waiting 24 hours before responding in any fashion.

- *Team orientation and delegation:* As noted, you were selected to lead the project because you demonstrated certain skills and qualities. Often, these were exhibited by you as an individual on a team. There are two things you need to remember. First, you are now the project manager and your job is not as an individual contributor of a specific piece of the project but rather your responsibility is to make sure all of the moving parts work together. Second, just as you will be developing professionally in certain areas on the project, so, too, will your team members. It might eat you up inside to see someone not doing as good a job as you would in a particular facet of the project, but your job is not to go in there and do it yourself but rather take the time to coach the individual so he or she can grow professionally in this particular area. You have to feel comfortable delegating.

TIP

You don't always know team members very well when starting a project. Hence, when delegating work on a project, start with small tasks to determine how well team members perform on delivering the required work. If they experience difficulties, take the time to coach them. This will benefit the project in the long run. As you gain confidence in their abilities, you can delegate more and larger tasks with a comfort level that the work will be completed.

- *Consistency:* You need to be consistent in the way you manage problems; deal with interpersonal issues; and treat your team members, clients, and others associated with the project.
- *Empathy:* Similar to consistency, you must exhibit empathy to those involved with the project. As much as you would like to

think that your project is the only thing your team members and clients are involved with, it is not. For you, as project manager, this might be the case. You need to respect that they have other responsibilities outside of the project. Exhibiting empathy often runs side by side with flexibility (see next point).

- *Flexibility:* Yes, you have a project plan to which you need to adhere. However, as contradictory as it sounds, you also need to be flexible. You need to be able to make trade-off decisions that ameliorate needs that are not directly related to the project (e.g., a colleague needs to "borrow" a resource for a short period to work on another project). When exhibiting flexibility, you need to make sure that you clearly specify the parameters involved. This will assure you that you can be flexible while at the same time not sacrifice the overall success of the project.

- *Follow through:* If you tell someone you are going to do something, then make sure you do it. It is important for the project that you continually instill confidence for all the key players. Lack of follow through will erode this confidence, having a devastating effect on the project.

- *Application-specific competence:* Believe it or not, this is not a necessary skill a good project manager needs to have—at least initially. A good project manager needs to develop an understanding of the underlying application area—whether it is technical (e.g., software, aerospace, telecommunications) or nontechnical (e.g., trade show, construction, real estate development)—but does not necessarily have to be a content expert in the underlying application at the inception of the project. If a project manager possesses the other skills listed here, he or she will be able to provide the "glue" necessary to bring a project in on time and on budget. The project manager will be able to pick up the application-specific competence along the way.

Whether you've managed projects before, or this is your first time managing a project, you will want to conduct a self-inventory of these skills and qualities.

TIP

When conducting a self-inventory of your skills and qualities that are required for successful project management, be hard on yourself. It is better for you to overcompensate in a specific area than undercompensate—undercompensating will compromise the confidence you will need to lead a successful project. Find a mentor—preferably outside your organization—to help you refine your self-inventory.

No one can say that he hasn't made mistakes in the past that need either to be rectified or that he does not want to repeat. You might assert, "Of course I have integrity!" But you have to put the project in the context in which it will be delivered. Perhaps you *personally* have integrity, but the department you are working in has had difficulty in the past—perception is reality. You may have to reestablish the integrity of the department because of problems in the past. After completing your self-inventory, select two or three areas you want to focus on as professional development areas.

The Skills and Qualities Self-Inventory is one way to obtain a snapshot of your self-evaluated skills and qualities *as they relate to the project* (remember the integrity example mentioned earlier). In Figure 8.2 we show a Skills and Qualities Self-Inventory completed by a project manager.

If you were a mentor, what areas would you recommend this project manager focus on during the project?

The Stakeholder Analysis Revisited

We talked extensively about the clients, sponsors, and other stakeholders earlier (see Table 6.6) when we were discussing the development of the Business Case, project buy-in, and clarification of needs and wants. Not only is the stakeholder analysis a technical tool used during the planning stage to determine the scope and work activities, but it also serves a

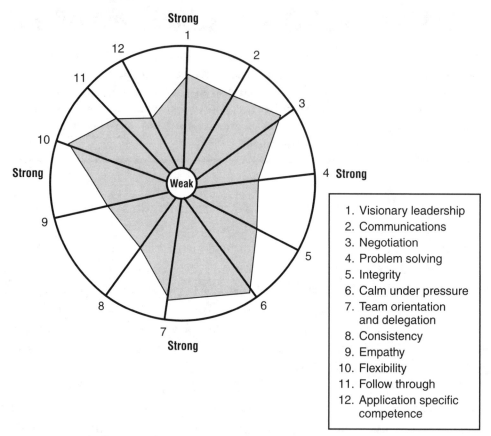

Figure 8.2 Skills and Qualities Self-Inventory. © Copyright 2007 Pamela McGhee and Peter McAliney.

major role in the Executing stage. In Execution, stakeholder analysis helps you organize your thoughts as a project manager about with whom you will communicate throughout the life of the project. While the technical component of the project at first glance appears to be the toughest part of the project, it is often managing the social aspects of the project—the people—that is the toughest.

Who Are You Really Managing?

The short answer is that you are managing more people than you think.

A priori, you have some relationship with all of the stakeholders, from no relationship at all to strong relationships that may have been developed over many years. In addition to the relationship you have with each individual associated with the project, individuals all have their own aspirations, skill sets, aptitudes, communication styles, learning styles, and motivations. What may be important to one may not be important to another. The more you know about the individuals' aspirations, skill sets, aptitudes, communication styles, learning styles, and motivations, the better you will be able to manage their expectations and contributions to the project.

At a very high level, you are managing your project team, your management team, your stakeholders, your clients, and your vendors. For each of these stakeholder groups—and individuals within each group—you will want to develop an overall picture of what "stake" each has in the project. The Individual Communication Plan (Table 8.1) can help you find out what makes each of the stakeholders tick.

You will probably want to try to fill out the Communications Plan, first, by yourself. Some of the categories are not relevant for all stakeholder groups (e.g., it is not that important to know the learning style for a vendor who is supplying you with a small item). You can also fill in some of the answers in the Plan—especially those that relate to your project team—by distributing a questionnaire or an online survey.

Once you have completed your initial pass at the Communications Plan, you probably will want to "road test" it with someone. Actually, you will want to road test it with more than one individual. Your choices here might be your mentor, a trusted colleague, a senior manager—anyone you feel can help you refine this very valuable information.

You will want to review portions of the Communications Plan (Table 8.1) with your project team.

TIP

Each project should serve as a professional development opportunity for each of the members of your team.

Table 8.1   Individual Communication Plan

Stakeholder Group	Individual	How to Communicate	How Often to Communicate	Importance of This Project
Project team	Person A			
	Person B			
	…			
	Person X			
Customer	Key contact A			
	Key contact B			
	…			
	Key contact X			
Sponsor	Sponsor A			
	Sponsor B			
	…			
	Sponsor X			
Company Managers	Functional			
	Geographical			
	…			
	Manager X			
Vendors/Suppliers	Vendor A			
	Vendor B			
	…			
	Vendor X			

Percent on This Project	Skill Sets	Aspirations	Communication Style	Learning Style	Motivation on Project

You will also want to find out what history exists between the individuals represented in the Stakeholder Chart (refer to Table 6.6 on pp. 154–155)—forewarned is forearmed. Do any of the individuals have a negative history? Do any of the individuals have a positive history? You want to know both, because in the former situation you want to avoid any potentially damaging conflicts and in the latter you want to take advantage of any leverage that you can employ right away. The more you know about the individuals associated with the project, the higher the likelihood of ultimate project success.

You will need to update the Individual Communication Plan as the project progresses through the different stages as players come and go. During the course of the project life, the nature and extent of the relationships between and among the different roles will manifest themselves in many different ways.

How Do You Manage

Once you have completed the initial stakeholder analysis, you can use the Stakeholder Chart (Table 6.6 on pp. 154–155) to determine the best way to manage all the stakeholders associated with your project. As a project manager, you are managing upward, downward, and laterally. Each requires a different style of management.

Here are some of the considerations that will guide you in managing the different stakeholders on the project:

- *Importance this project:* How important is this project to each of the stakeholders?
  - —*Stakeholders considered:* Project team, company managers, clients, vendors
  - —Very often different stakeholders place a different level of importance to the project as it relates to other work in which they are involved. Knowing what priority a stakeholder places on your project will help you manage expectations.

- *Percent this project:* What percent of the stakeholders' time is devoted to this project?

  —*Stakeholders considered:* Project team, clients, vendors

  —For stakeholders with a small percent of time devoted to your project, you need to be cognizant of their other commitments so that when you reach the invariable crunch times, you frame your request for their time in a manner that is respectful of their other commitments.

- *Skill sets:* What skill sets does each stakeholder bring to the project?

  —*Stakeholders considered:* Project team, clients

  —Having an appropriate awareness of your project team and client team skill sets is important to help you manage your expectations.

- *Aspirations:* How will this project experience serve each stakeholder's longer-term goals?

  —*Stakeholders considered:* Project team, company managers, clients, vendors

  —Each stakeholder has a continuum that defines his career. Your project is one point of that continuum. The more you know about how each stakeholder views your project in his personal continuum, the more likely you will be to have him contribute the most he can to the project.

- *Communications style:* What is the preferred communication style of each stakeholder—how does she like to communicate?

  —*Stakeholders considered:* Project team, company managers, clients, vendors

  —It is important to know how individuals like to communicate. Some are verbally oriented and like to discuss things in person and on the phone while others are more visually oriented and like to read memos, e-mails, and reports. Knowing this in advance will help you allocate your time.

- *Learning style:* What is the preferred learning style of each stakeholder—how does he or she like to learn?

  —*Stakeholders considered:* Project team, clients

  —Each project represents a learning opportunity for all involved. You as a project manager, however, need to be acutely aware of the learning styles of those who are "in the trenches" completing the work on the project—that is, your direct project and client team.

TIP

To learn more about learning styles, look to the frameworks established by Kolb, Gardner, and Dunn & Dunn. Additional areas to consult would be theories on life-long learning, learning literacy, and continuing education.[1]

- *Motivation:* What makes each stakeholder tick?

  —*Stakeholders considered:* Project team, company managers, clients, vendors

  —As a project manager, you need to inspire individuals on your work team to exert high levels of effort to achieve the project's— and ultimately the organization's—goals.

Armed with this individual stakeholder information, the more general stakeholder analysis, the Strategic Communications Plan, and the Operating Communications Plan, you now have the tools to manage all facets of communications on the project.

Team Life Cycle

As project manager, you will be assembling your team. Your team, as we acknowledged earlier, is not only your immediate project team, but also includes, in varying degrees, vendors, clients, and company managers (i.e., the project stakeholders). It would be wonderful if we were able to select everyone that is on our team, but we know that usually is not the case. To configure the individuals who have been assigned to the project team into a *true* project team, you must go through a standard life cycle of forming, storming, norming, performing, and adjourning.[2] Different management styles are required in each of the defined phases.

Forming

Forming is the first phase. Before a team forms, individuals will have a varying level of familiarity with the other team members (from no familiarity to having worked closely together in the past). The team has to get to know each other and they will jointly discuss what the specific project is about, what the context of the project is, and what potential challenges might exist. They will discuss their objectives and goals both individually and as a team. They will discuss how they want to address the work.

Team members tend to be quite polite and civil to each other in the forming stage. They tend to be individually focused at this point and it is unclear to the project manager what motivates each of the team members. As the team forms, it is often helpful to share the Team Life Cycle model with the team members so they are aware of the journey they will be taking together. From a project management persepctive, you will want to be directive in your management style in the forming stage. You want to make sure all of the individuals joining the team start off by being pointed in the same direction.

Storming

Storming is the second phase in the Team Life Cycle. In this phase, individuals start to assert themselves and try to establish the best position for themselves in the team. As such, it can get quite contentious.

Differences of opinion emerge and team members confront each other on their respective positions.

TIP

By opening up the vocabulary of the Team Life Cycle to your team during the forming stage, you can avert disaster in the storming stage. If storming occurs, encourage team members who are not in the middle of the storm to work through calming those who are. This can potentially avoid a disastrous situation.

Storming, while sounding nothing short of disastrous, is a necessary stage in the Team Life Cycle. While a team is storming, all of its energies are directed at the unproductive activity of the internal storm—not working toward completing the project goal. Similar to the way an individual emerges from a period of hardship stronger, a team will emerge stronger when it emerges from the storming phase—*if* it emerges from the storming phase. A more seasoned team of individuals has a much higher probability of passing through the storming phase in a short period of time. From a project management perspective, you still want to be directive in your management style as you help team members navigate the rough waters of the storming stage.

Norming

Norming is the third phase. During norming the team starts to work as a team. Productivity begins to increase because individuals have worked out how they will work together. Routines are established and territories will have been marked. Trust begins to be established and this, in turn, will increase individual motivation toward accomplishing the goal of the team.

As project manager, you need to be on the alert that teams do not become too complacent during the norming phase. If so, they may engage in counterproductive activities such as group think and "analysis by paralysis." The management style you want to exhibit during norming is participative—you have developed a trust that your team has taken responsibility for parts of the project that they have taken ownershiip of. You rely on them as professionals to get the job done.

Performing

Performing is the fourth stage. It is in this stage when productivity is at its greatest. Team members are interdependent, are motivated, and know exactly what they—and their teammates—need to do to be successful as a team. Team members have exhibited their abiltiy to make independent decisions for the good of the team so artificial decision-making hurdles have been eliminated. Project managers display a participative mangement style in the performing stage.

Adjourning and Transforming

Adjourning and transforming is the fifth and final stage. It corresponds to the Project Close. In addition to closing the project from a technical perspective, the project manager should take the time during this phase to review her own profesional development goals and those of her team. Here, the project manager exhibits a transformational management style.

TIP

As project manager, you mustn't get too complacent about your team. Teams can move backward through the Team Life Cycle, especially when new members join the team or there is a change in key personnel in one of the stakeholder groups.

Figure 8.3 shows the associated productivity of a team during the Team Life Cycle.

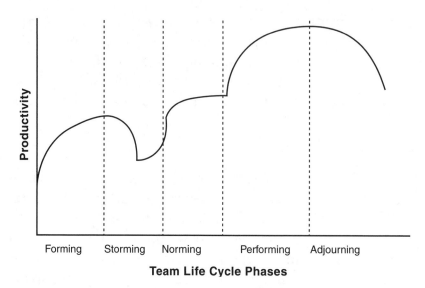

Figure 8.3   Productivity during the Team Life Cycle. © Copyright 2007 Pamela McGhee and Peter McAliney.

Team Types

A project team in essence is a work team. As such, the goals of the project team will be accomplished through the collective performance of the team. There will be created, as the team goes through the Team Life Cycle, a collective synergy that allows the team to accomplish more than the individual parts if added up. Accountability will be both individual and mutual because it is the team that delivers the end product. Skills on the team will be complementary, thus enabling individuals to both contribute from their area of expertise while at the same time learn other skills from their team members.

There are four types of team structures that can be employed in project management:

1. *Hierarchical structured team:* A hierarchical structured team is usually organized along functional lines (Figure 8.4). Here your role as project manager is very clear because issues such as au-

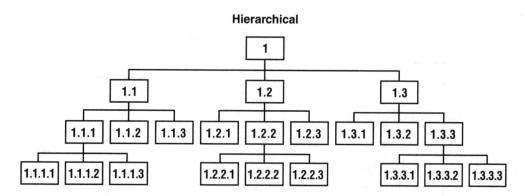

Figure 8.4 Hierarchical Team Structure. © Copyright 2007 Pamela McGhee and Peter McAliney.

thority, decision making, leadership, and interactions among team members are very clear. This kind of team is usually only applicable to projects with a relatively narrow scope.

2. *Matrix structured or project matrix team:* A matrix structure team involves lines of authority from at least two areas (Figure 8.5). These areas could be functional, geographic, business unit, or end user customer. Managing a matrix team presents challenges for a project manager in that he or she must often time share a resource with others. Additionally, if the project manager is not responsible for the individual's performance review, he or she may exert less control on a project team member.

3. *Tiger team:* A tiger team is a virtual team that remains in its home organization (Figure 8.6). They come together to work on a particular project while still carrying out responsibilities in their home organization. While the strength of a tiger team is the vast number of skills and perspectives that are brought to a project, it is a difficult team to manage for similar reasons that are associated with the matrix team.

4. *Skunk works:* A skunk works team draws individuals from different parts of the organization and separates them out of the

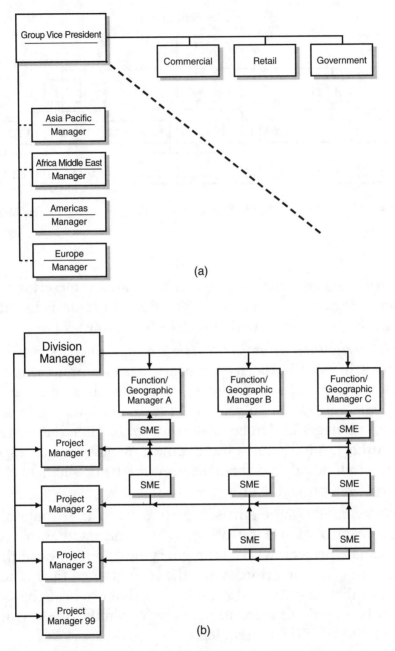

Figure 8.5 Project Matrix Team (a) Matrix Structured (b) Project Structured. © Copyright 2007 Pamela McGhee and Peter McAliney.

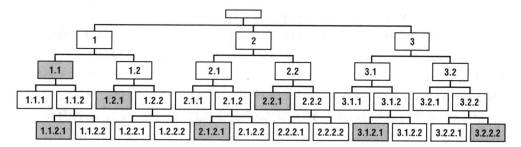

Figure 8.6 Tiger Team. © Copyright 2007 Pamela McGhee and Peter McAliney.

mainstream (Figure 8.7). This works well in addressing projects that are not in the company's main line of work. A skunk works team has the potential to take longer to go through the Team Life Cycle than other kinds of teams but is very powerful once it emerges from the storming phase.

Note on Politics

Politics exist in any organization. Because as a project manager you are managing up, down, and laterally, your ability to navigate the political quagmires both within and across organizations is an essential skill you must master. You will want to keep this in mind as you develop your Strategic Communications Plan. You will want to determine who your allies are and what you need to do to support your allies.

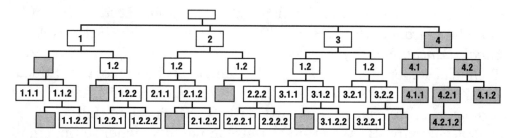

Figure 8.7 Skunk Works. © Copyright 2007 Pamela McGhee and Peter McAliney.

Similarly, you will need to identify those who may provide resistance to completing your job. For these individuals (often called negative stakeholders), you will need to make a determination if you will be able to turn them into allies or settle for knowing that there is nothing in your control to convert them. If an individual falls into the latter category, you will want to develop strategies to neutralize the influence he or she has on key decision makers and stakeholders associated with the project.

Conclusion

Managing a project team requires attention to the technical details of the project as well as the "care and feeding" of the different stakeholder groups associated with the project. It is as important to keep the goal of the project first and foremost as it is to make sure that you remain attentive to all of the vagaries associated with the process of completing the project. There are technical elements and there are social elements—you need to make sure both are addressed in order to ensure your success.

Notes

1. Dunn, R. S., & Dunn, K. J. (1979). Learning styles/teaching styles: Should they . . . can they . . . be matched? *Educational Leadership, 36*(4), 238–244; Gardner, H., & Hatch, T. (1990). *Multiple intelligences go to school: Educational implications of the theory of multiple intelligences.* (Technical Report No. 4). New York: Center for Technology in Education; Kolb, D. A. (1984). *Experiential learning: Experience as a source of learning and development.* Engelwood Cliffs, NJ: Prentice Hall.

2. Tuckman, B. W. (1965). Developmental sequence in small groups. *Psychological Bulletin, 63,* 384–399.

REAL LIFE EXPERIENCES FROM THE TRENCHES

VIGNETTE 8—The Early Bird Gets the Worm

A billion-dollar project to design and build a Saudi Arabian defense system had been canceled due to poor project management and delivery. The next contender—a contractor—would need to convince the overseeing body, the U.S. Air Force, that they could deliver the project under an accelerated schedule. To sweeten the deal, the Air Force and the Saudi government threw in a $50 million bonus for delivering the project ahead of schedule. On the downside, delivering the project late could result in liquidated damages for as much as $50 million. The Saudi project became the most important project in the corporation.

The project manager was well liked and respected by both senior management and the staff. A slowdown of project starts in this particular division of the corporation enabled him to handpick talented staff for the project. Unfortunately, the team had a problem similar to that of the U.S. Olympic Basketball Team—many stars but not quite a team. In an early staff meeting, one of the engineers on the project complained, "these projects would be easy to manage if we could just eliminate the people." The project manager had his work cut out for him.

With over 500 people working on the project, there was a constant stream of people issues to deal with including getting "big" personalities to work together, replacing or backing up individuals who had personal problems, key players being removed from the project at critical times to support other projects, and dealing with infighting among staff members. Clearly the project manager could not deal with all of the people issues on a personal basis, but he wanted to ensure that people issues were dealt with well and that he would be accessible to support all areas of the program to deal with both technical and organizational issues. The project manager instituted a meeting process that fit the bill, the daily "Early Bird" meeting.

Every morning at 7:30 A.M. all of the project manager's direct reports and staff attended a 30-minute meeting called the "Early Bird." At this meeting, all of the key issues and actions were discussed in a staccato style. The meeting was attended by a little more than a dozen people. It ended promptly at 8:00 A.M. A critical point of the meeting was near the end when the project manager would ask every individual—one at a time—whether he or she had *any* issue that needed to be discussed or brought to the project manager's attention. "No surprises" was the hallmark of the project manager's management style and the project. The entire management team quickly came to realize that this was the meeting that created the cohesion across the project. People issues were dealt with head-on in these meetings. A tribute to the project manager, the all-star team jelled quickly and followed the project manager's keen leadership.

In retrospect, the "Early Bird" meeting seems so simple a solution to getting a team on track for people issues. In setting a tone and energy level every morning while enabling an open communication at the beginning of each day across all functions, the project team went on to deliver what the Air Force deemed "the most successful program in Air Force history." With demonstrated leadership and people skills, the project manager went on to become the CEO. The "Early Bird" was adopted as a standard meeting for all projects.

BRIAN HAGEN
Strategic Capabilities, Inc.

We hope that this slim volume has helped bring some order and simplicity to project management for you.

Our templates are available, free of charge, on the web at http://www.painlessprojectmanagement.info. We update our templates from time to time, so visit us often at our site.

PAMELA MCGHEE and PETER MCALINEY

Template 1
Project Context Diagram

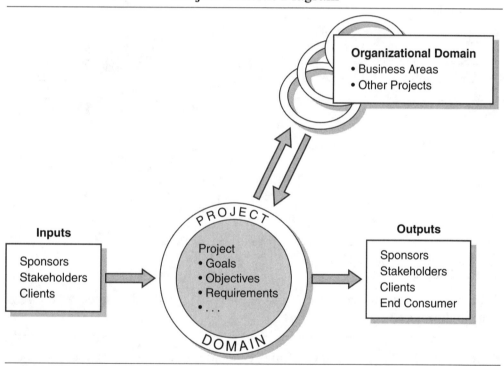

Template 2
Needs and Wants Template

Needs versus Wants List   Date: _____
Sponsor: _____

Needs: Wants:
1. _____ $ _____   +   1. _____ $ _____
2. _____ $ _____   2. _____ $ _____
3. _____ $ _____   3. _____ $ _____
Total = $ _____   Total = $ _____

Stakeholder 1: _____

Needs: Wants:
1. _____ $ _____   +   1. _____ $ _____
2. _____ $ _____   2. _____ $ _____
3. _____ $ _____   3. _____ $ _____
Total = $ _____   Total = $ _____

Stakeholder N: _____

Needs: Wants:
1. _____ $ _____   +   1. _____ $ _____
2. _____ $ _____   2. _____ $ _____
3. _____ $ _____   3. _____ $ _____
Total = $ _____   Total = $ _____
Grand Total = $ _____   Grand Total = $ _____

Minimum budget and scope for   Maximum budget and scope for
potential project   potential project

Template 3
Business Case Outline

Business Case Overview
    Proposed project
    Principal investigator(s)
    Contributors
    Project mission

Proposed Project Details
    The issue or problem to be addressed/solved
    The goals and benefits of undertaking such a project
    The objectives of the project
    The needs and wants
    The potential project scope
    The risks and impacts associated with the project
    The cost benefit analysis
    The return on investment (ROI)

How the Project Supports
    Corporate vision/mission
    Corporate goals and objectives
    Division goals and objectives
    Functional goals and objectives
    Project portfolio (if applicable)

Feedback Requested
    Areas for clarification
    Decision

Template 4
The Integrated Project Plan (Short Version)

Project Charter (Statement of Scope or Project Scope Document)
- Risk identification
- Assumptions
- Constraints
- Primary project driver
- List of stakeholders

Work Breakdown Structure (WBS) to the Task Level
- Risk planning/mitigation

Logic Diagram
- Network
- Event/precedence

Gantt Chart
- Schedule (Time and labor costs)

Cost Spreadsheet (Nonlabor Costs Associated with Tasks)

© Copyright 2007 Pamela McGhee and Peter McAliney. To customize this document, download it to your hard drive from www.painlessprojectmanagement.info. The document can then be opened, edited, and printed using Microsoft Word.

Template 5
Project Charter Template

Project Charter: Sample Outline for Smaller Projects

Project Mission Statement

- Articulated link to corporate mission statement
- Articulated link to division mission statement

Project Goal Statement

Statement of Scope (can include a visualization)

Project Objectives

Critical Success Factors

Critical Success Measures

List of Relevant Risks

List of Assumptions

Project Constraints

Primary Project Driver

Identification of All

- Stakeholders
- Sponsors
- Clients
- Other interested parties

Template 6
A WBS Can Be Oganized by Work Cycle

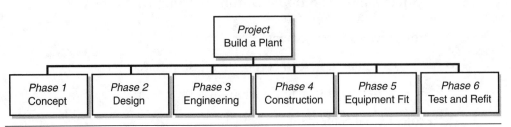

Template 7
A WBS Can Be Organized by Content or Subject Matter

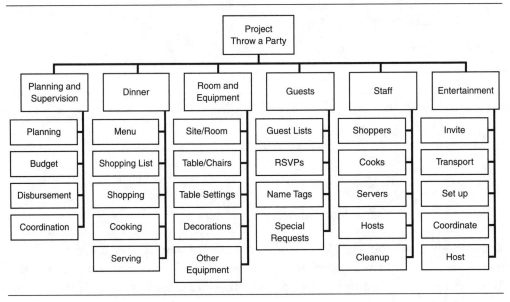

Template 8
A WBS Can Be Organized According to Deliverables

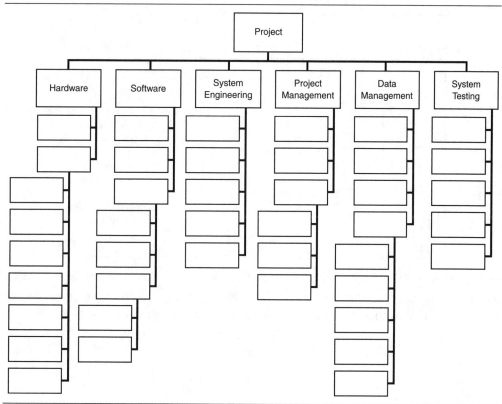

Template 9
A Leveled WBS

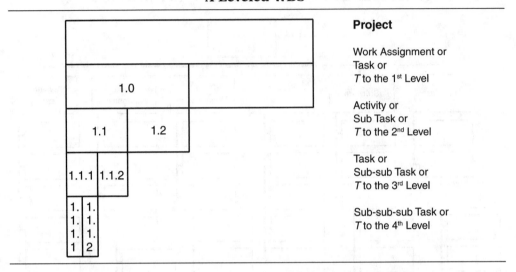

	Project
1.0	Work Assignment or Task or *T* to the 1st Level
1.1 1.2	Activity or Sub Task or *T* to the 2nd Level
1.1.1 1.1.2	Task or Sub-sub Task or *T* to the 3rd Level
	Sub-sub-sub Task or *T* to the 4th Level

Template 10
Work Breakdown Structure

Project							
Work Assignment				Work Assignment (Large task)			
Activity		Activity		Activity		Activity	
Task	Task	Task	Task	Task	Task	Task	(Small task)

APPENDIX

224

Template 11
Gantt Chart Showing Calendar Duration

Task	Resource	1	2	3	4	5	6
			Weeks				
A	Paula	4.36 da					
B	Jerry		1.45 da				
C	Paula		4.36 da				
D	Jane		2.90 da				
E	Steve		7.27 da				
F	Bob				8.72 da		
G	Jerry				5.81 da		
H	Paula					4.36 da	

Day 23

Template 12
Stakeholder Analysis Chart

Stakeholder Group	Individual	Potential Issues	Potential Conflicts with Other Stakeholders
Project team	Person A		
	Person B		
	...		
	Person X		
Customer	Key contact A		
	Key contact B		
	...		
	Key contact X		
Sponsor	Sponsor A		
	Sponsor B		
	...		
	Sponsor X		
Company managers	Functional		
	Geographical		
	...		
	Manager X		
Vendors/suppliers	Vendor A		
	Vendor B		
	...		
	Vendor X		

Template 13
Step 1 Risk Identification Chart

Risk Category	Project Risk	Probability
Project	1…	M
		H
	N…	L
Partner	1…	L
		H
	N…	H
Business	1…	M
		M
	N…	M
External	1…	L
		L
	N…	H

© Copyright 2007 Pamela McGhee and Peter McAliney. To customize this document, download it to your hard drive from www.painlessprojectmanagement.info. The document can then be opened, edited, and printed using Microsoft Word.

Template 14
Sample Responsibility-Accountability Map

Deliverable/Project Member	Price Quote	Advertising Schedule	Station Demos	Program Schedule	Other Advertisers	Contract
Recording engineer	—	—	—	—	C	—
Marketing assistant	R	R	P	R	R	I
Product manager	A	S	R	S	S	A
Division manager	I	I	S	I	I	R
Research and development	—	—	—	—	I	—
Publicity	—	—	—	I	I	—
Legal	—	—	—	—	—	S
Controller	—	—	—	—	—	S

Note: P = Participates; A = Assists; R = Responsible; S = Sign-off; I = Communications/FYI only.

© Copyright 2007 Pamela McGhee and Peter McAliney. To customize this document, download it to your hard drive from www.painlessprojectmanagement.info. The document can then be opened, edited, and printed using Microsoft Word.

Template 15
Stakeholder Chart—Strategic Communications Plan

Stakeholder Group	Individual	Potential Issues	Probability Issues May Arise
Project team	Person A		
	Person B		
	…		
	Person X		
Customer	Key contact A		
	Key contact B		
	…		
	Key contact X		
Sponsor	Sponsor A		
	Sponsor B		
	…		
	Sponsor X		
Company managers	Functional		
	Geographical		
	…		
	Manager X		
Vendors/suppliers	Vendor A		
	Vendor B		
	…		
	Vendor X		

Impact of Not Addressing Issue	Response to Potential Issue	How Often to Communicate	How to Communicate

Template 16
Elevator Report

Prepared by: _____

Activity Category	Completion Status			
	Ahead/On/Behind Schedule	Ahead/On/Behind Budget	Date Close	Critical Path (Y/N)
Significant accomplishments for current period				
Significant accomplishments for upcoming period				

Date: _____

Stakeholders Directly Impacted	Accomplishment	Notes	Responsible

(continued)

Template 16 *(Continued)*

Completion Status				
Activity Category	Date Reported	Date Due	Date Close	Critical Path (Y/N)
Open issues closed from prior period				
Open issues Remaining from prior period			Open	
			Open	
			Open	
			Open	
			Open	
			Open	
New issues added for current period			Open	
			Open	
			Open	
			Open	
			Open	
			Open	

Stakeholders Directly Impacted	Issue	Notes	Responsible

Template 17
Change Request Form

Project Name _____	Change Tracking No. _____
Requestor name _____ Contact info _____ Date requested _____	
Approved (Y/N)	Date approved _____

To be completed by requestor
Description of change _____

_____

Reason for change _____

_____

Anticipated impact to project if change not undertaken _____

_____

_____

Anticipated impact to other parts of project if change is made _____

_____

_____

Alternatives to undertake if change is not possible _____

_____

_____

Estimated additional time and cost to effect change _____

_____

_____

_____

Template 17 *(Continued)*

Estimated additional time and cost to effect change _____

_____

_____

_____

To be completed by project manager

Relevant comments on:

- Not undertaking change
- Impact to other parts
- Alternatives

Recommendation to Change Board _____

To be completed by Change Board

Decision _____

Template 18
Individual Communication Plan

Stakeholder Group	Individual	How to Communicate	How Often to Communicate	Importance of This Project
Project team	Person A			
	Person B			
	…			
	Person X			
Customer	Key contact A			
	Key contact B			
	…			
	Key contact X			
Sponsor	Sponsor A			
	Sponsor B			
	…			
	Sponsor X			
Company Managers	Functional			
	Geographical			
	…			
	Manager X			
Vendors/Suppliers	Vendor A			
	Vendor B			
	…			
	Vendor X			

Percent on This Project	Skill Sets	Aspirations	Communication Style	Learning Style	Motivation on Project